John Stott: Big Ideas and an Adventure of Faith

This book helps you understand Uncle John's life in a friendly way. We read it in our Bible Breakfast Club on Saturday mornings, and we discussed it together. It was really fun.
Peter Tice
London, UK

Truly one of the best books I have ever read. I've enjoyed it 12 times cover to cover. Uncle John's faith in God when things looked impossible amazed me. I know you will love it too.
Willow Rinehart
California, USA

This story will introduce you to 'Uncle John' in a way that is not only enjoyable but fascinating. You may find it hard to put down, as I did. I hope you will want to explore more of John Stott's life as the years pass, and that you will discover his books, too, all written in the service of the Lord Jesus Christ. Here in Julia Cameron's fresh and engaging style and format 'Uncle John' is vividly portrayed.
Bishop Timothy Dudley-Smith
John Stott's authorized biographer

John Stott: Big Ideas and an Adventure of Faith

Authorized biography for children and children-at-heart

Julia Cameron

In association with

Evangelical Fellowship in
the Anglican Communion

With thankfulness to God
for the ministries of
John Stott and Frances Whitehead

Dictum Press
Oxford UK
www.dictumpress.com

ISBN 978 1 83809 724 0
All rights reserved

This edition © Dictum Press 2021

Copyright © Julia E M Cameron

Design and illustrations by Rebecca J Hall
rebeccajhall.co.uk

Originally published in the UK in 2012, reprinted 2016
by Christian Focus Publications under the title
John Stott: The Humble Leader

A catalogue record for this book is available from the British Library

Printed by TJ Books, UK

Acknowledgements

I gained much from John Stott's earlier biographers, particularly Timothy Dudley-Smith who compiled a masterful authorized biography in two volumes, carefully-annotated. I also appreciated Chris Wright's gathered reminiscences from a few of Uncle John's friends, published for his 90th birthday.

In addition, several people whose names appear in this book have given me their personal memories, and introduced me to others who could reconstruct episodes from decades ago.

Frances Whitehead (1925-2019), John Stott's Secretary for 55 years, brought her characteristic encouragement along the way, and very kindly read the full manuscript to ensure it brought an accurate portrayal of Uncle John's life. Frances was able to read parts of this story to John in 2011, as the writing was completed about a month before he died.

The book has been considerably re-shaped since its first edition, and I'm grateful for the imagination Rebecca J Hall has brought to this.

The contributors share a hope that children who come to know more about Uncle John from this book will go on to appreciate and be inspired by some of his extensive writing.

Julia E M Cameron
Oxford, January 2021

The facts in this book are all true. Some pieces of conversation are recorded as they happened; other pieces have been imagined, in order to tell the story

Contents

Timeline 9

Start Here 13

1. Early years in Harley Street 15
2. Off to school 21
3. A student in Cambridge 39
4. Pacifism and war 43
5. Training for the church at Ridley Hall 51
6. A curate becomes homeless 59
7. All Souls Rector 69
8. Escaping to The Hookses 85
9. Students, students and more students! 93
10. The worldwide church 109
11. Focus on the Lausanne Movement 117
12. John Stott: the man himself 125
13. And finally 135

Appendices 137

   Questions for book clubs 138

   Three ideas of things to do 141

Timeline

1921	John Robert Walmsley Stott, born in London on Wednesday 27 April. Baptized in Marylebone Parish Church
1927-1929	King Arthur's School, Kensington
1929-1935	Oakley Hall School, Cirencester
1935-1940	Rugby School
1940-1944	Trinity College, Cambridge
1944-1945	Ridley Hall, Cambridge
1945-1950	Curate, All Souls, Langham Place
1950-1975	Rector, All Souls, Langham Place, then Rector Emeritus
1951	Shaped new direction of World Evangelical Fellowship
1956	Appointed Frances Whitehead as his secretary
1959–1991	Chaplain to the Queen, then Extra Chaplain to the Queen
1961	Founded the Evangelical Fellowship in the Anglican Communion (EFAC)
1967	First UK National Evangelical Anglican Congress (NEAC)
1969	Founded Langham Trust

1971	Founded Evangelical Literature Trust, which became part of Langham Partnership International
1974	Lausanne Congress on World Evangelization. Chief Architect of The Lausanne Covenant
1975	Established first London Lectures in Contemporary Christianity. (Now the John Stott London Lectures)
1979+	Vice-President then Ambassador-at-Large, International Fellowship of Evangelical Students (IFES)
1982	Founded the London Institute for Contemporary Christianity (LICC) in St Peter's Vere Street
1983	Received Lambeth DD
1989	Second Lausanne Congress on World Evangelization. Chief Architect of The Manila Manifesto
1991	Two books specially published for 70th birthday (UK and USA)
2002	Founded Langham Partnership International
2004	Made lifelong Honorary Chairman, Lausanne Movement
2005	Included in *TIME* magazine's list of '100 most influential people'
2006	Awarded CBE in Queen's New Year's Honours list
2007	Moved into the College of St Barnabas
2010	Published his final book *The Radical Disciple* to say goodbye to his readers
2011	*A Portrait by his Friends* published to mark 90th birthday; John Stott dies on 27 July; his ashes are buried in Dale churchyard, close to The Hookses
2012	Memorial service in St Paul's Cathedral, 13 January

Map of Central London

John Stott's London. These places are within walking distance. This simplified map will help you find them.

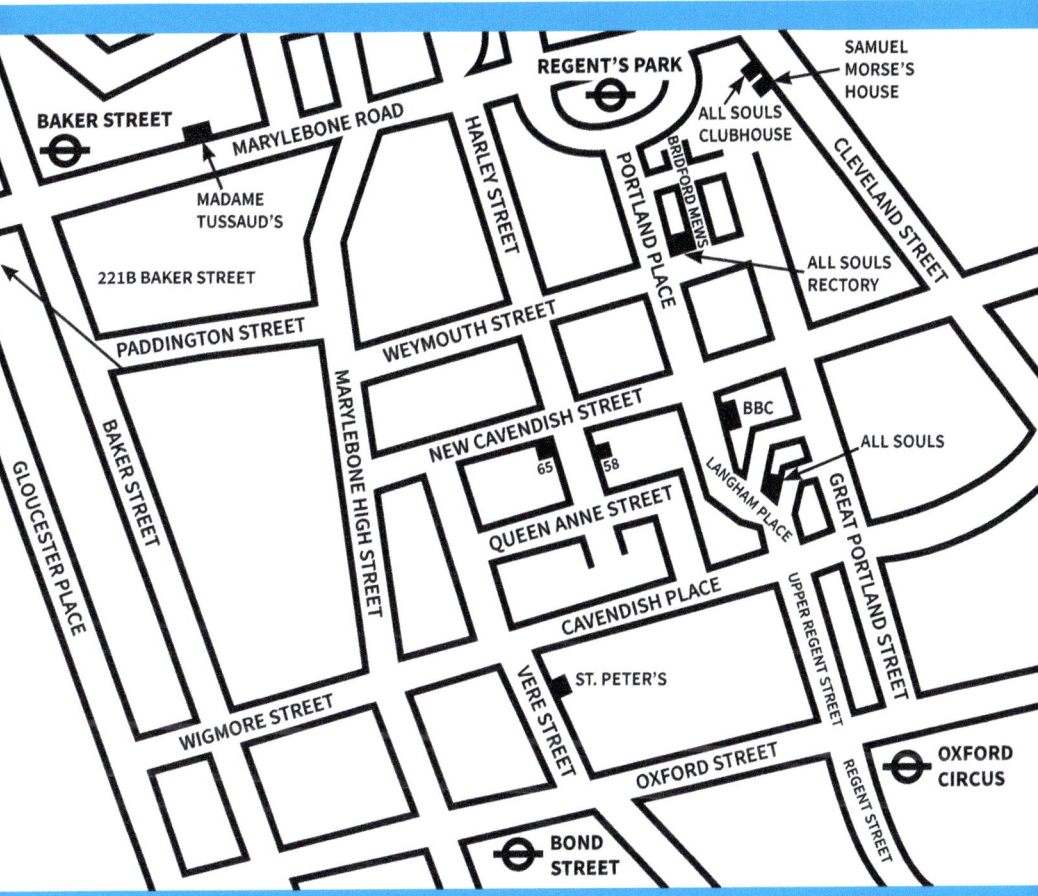

Map is not to scale

Start Here

John Stott had friends all over the world, as he travelled widely. Most of them knew him as 'Uncle John'. As you learn more about him, you may begin to think of him as 'Uncle John' too. He liked to be called that by people who got to know him.

In April 2005, Uncle John's name appeared in the American magazine *TIME*, and it took everyone by surprise.

Picture a group of his friends in an airport or a railway station in London, or New York, or Sydney or Singapore or Nairobi. One of them has just bought a copy of *TIME* from the news stand. This is what you might have heard.

Ben Look at this! Uncle John's here!

Grace Where?

Ben Here in *TIME*. He's listed as one of the '100 most influential people in the world'!

Everyone else Let's see! Wow! I can't believe that! You're kidding us!

Femi Yes, there he is - with Barack Obama, Bill Gates, Oprah Winfrey.

Jemima Did you know his father handed him some cyanide when he was about six?

Everyone else What??!!

Jemima Truly, he *did*. Uncle John told me! It could have killed him!

Ben I remember someone saying he became a tramp in London.

Grace A tramp? I thought he was a Chaplain to the Queen.

[Both were true, but who would believe that?]

Femi Did you hear how he went to Sunday School with daggers down his socks? Dressed to kill, you could say!

[They all laughed]

Grace Just think, if people used all the titles they were given, Uncle John would be called The Revd Dr Dr Dr Dr Dr Dr John Stott CBE. He received *six* doctorates.

And so they shared their stories, and they laughed out loud, as some of the stories were very funny.

When you reach the end of this book, you will know quite a lot about John Stott. You will see why he was in the 'Top 100' list of influential people.

We have packed all we can into these pages, but there is much more to tell. To delve further, you will find a list of things you can do on page 141.

John Stott was driven by a passion for Jesus Christ's name to be honoured around the world. He described himself as 'a pastor, leader and friend'. While highly gifted, as is evident from his story, he was a humble man.

As Hebrews 13:7 says
**Remember your leaders, who spoke the word of God to you.
Consider the outcome of their way of life and imitate their faith.**

John Stott gave towering leadership to the church for over half a century, in a gracious and humble way. Let's consider the outcome of his way of life, and imitate his faith.

So we begin at the beginning, in London, a long time ago.

Chapter 1

Early Years in Harley Street

May 1921

'Do hurry up, darling!' Joanna's mother called up the stairs.

'Just coming!' Joanna's stuff was all over the floor, so she closed her bedroom door behind her, then ran down the stairs. Most of her things were packed, apart from the last few books and jigsaws. Joanna Stott was excited as she sat down to breakfast. Moving house was an adventure, even if she was moving only a couple of miles. Ever since she heard about it, she had been impatiently planning her new room.

Breakfast was almost finished when the removal men knocked on the door. With four in the team they made fast progress. Soon pictures were being taken off the walls, rooms were gradually emptied of furniture, and carpets were rolled up. While Joanna was excited, her little sister Joy cried. Joy's toys were being packed into boxes and she wanted them back.

With a nine-year-old trying to help but getting too excited, and a toddler crying, it seemed best for both of them, and their baby brother, John, to be taken out to the park. John was less than a month old, and went off to sleep as soon as his nanny began to push the pram.

By mid-afternoon, the removal van was parked outside the Stotts' new house: 58 Harley Street, one of the best-known streets in central London.

'Bring the carpets off first,' said the chief removal man. 'We'll lay them down, then tackle the furniture.' Dr Stott was in charge of what went into his consulting room and Mrs Stott supervised the rest of the house. Joanna would soon be arranging her new room.

Number 58 Harley Street was a tall, narrow building, on six floors, with servants' quarters in the basement. Dr Stott's consulting room was on the ground floor, next to the family dining room, which had to double as a waiting room. Each day, as soon as lunch was over, the domestic staff quickly cleared the table, and placed the chairs along the sides of the room. Appointments started at 2pm, and people often came early.

Joy and John shared a nursery on the third floor where they spent much of the day. They played games, had fun, and fought and argued. Joy was two years older than John, but she didn't have the upper hand for long. 'Are they twins?' people often asked when they were out. John was tall, and Joy less tall for her age. Children always like to be thought of as older than they are, so John liked to be taken for Joy's twin. Joy definitely didn't like it! John was soon taller than Joy, and then people assumed he was the older one.

About four years before he was born, John's parents had suffered a deep tragedy. For there had been a third older sister, Rosemary, nicknamed Tubby, who died. Every year on the anniversary of Rosemary's birthday, John's mother would place a sprig of the herb rosemary on each of the children's desks. This little one was remembered with deep affection by her parents, and by her older sister Joanna.

The children's nanny read them stories, taught them numbers, and helped them to tie their shoelaces and learn to tell the time. In the afternoons she took them to play in Park Square Gardens at the top of Harley Street. These gardens were private, but all householders in the area had a key to unlock their iron gates. The gardens were very well kept, and the children needed to behave in a demure way. As John got older, he did not always do that. All his life he kept a letter which was sent to his father when he was aged eight. This letter, from the Clerk to the Board of the Crown Estate Paving Commission, complained of John's 'unruly behaviour' and urged Arnold Stott to keep his son under better control.

Sometimes, the children's nanny took them across Marylebone Road into Regents Park, which is the home of London Zoo. Every season brought its beauty, and the children loved the expanse of lawns and playing hide-and-seek in the rhododendron dens. In the winter the lake could freeze hard enough for people to skate across it. In Regents Park they occasionally caught sight of the young princesses, Elizabeth and Margaret, being driven around the park inner circle. Elizabeth would be crowned Queen Elizabeth II at the age of 26. She was just five years younger than John.

Having a nanny to look after children was common for Harley Street families. The Stott children loved their nanny, whom they called Nanny Golden, and she kept in touch with the family long after the children grew up. Nanny Golden was a Christian, and she no doubt prayed for the children to come to faith themselves. She taught them children's hymns and choruses, and John and Joy would sing these with enthusiasm.

Like most children, John developed a special fondness for animals. When he was about two, he was chasing a squirrel in the park to give it with some bread. He fell over, and the squirrel vanished. His sister Joanna tells us what happened next. 'John picked himself up and said "poor squirrel". Well, actually he inserted a swear word in the middle – having heard it somewhere and with no idea what it might mean! I think our nanny was a bit shocked. We laughed about it for years!'

From when John was small, his father enjoyed the chance to take him on walks. Arnold Stott wanted to help him appreciate and enjoy all the animal life, plant life and bird life around him, and to learn more about them. John loved these walks, hand-in-hand with his father. 'John, shut your mouth and open your eyes and ears!' his father said. 'It's the only way to observe nature.'

On Sunday mornings, Nanny Golden took John and Joy to All Souls Church in Langham Place. They sat in the front of the balcony, one each side of her, so they didn't misbehave. But you cannot stop inventive children from misbehaving. During the prayers, they ransacked their pockets for any bus tickets or other scraps of paper, screwed them into pellets and dropped them on the hats of the unsuspecting ladies seated below. Then they would duck back quickly.

John was full of fun ideas. One Sunday, as the service reached the Lord's Prayer and Nanny Golden leaned forward to pray, a new idea struck him.

From behind Nanny Golden's back, Joy suddenly saw John's hand appear, holding his school cap upside down. 'Collection please,' he whispered, with his voice as low as it could go. Joy burst into uncontrollable giggles.

Undeterred by their morning performance, Nanny Golden took the children to Sunday School in the afternoons. The Sunday School was held in the All Souls Rectory at 12 Weymouth Street. John never behaved well, and most weeks he was sent out of the classroom for bad behaviour soon after the lesson began. In fact he spent more time outside the classroom than inside! He went to Sunday School armed with toy daggers stuck into his socks, and an imitation revolver in his belt to scare the girls. His Sunday School teachers probably despaired of him.

Fascinating Fact 1

JOHN ARRIVES IN THE FAMILY

John was born on 27 April 1921, the Stotts' fourth child and first son. His father had grown up in Bolton, outside Manchester, in the north of England, where John's grandfather owned a cotton mill.

Baby John was baptized shortly after the family moved to Harley Street, in nearby Marylebone Church. His full name was John Robert Walmsley Stott, after his paternal grandfather John Robert Stott, with the addition of Walmsley from his mother Lily's family line.

John's father Arnold Stott was a heart specialist. It is still said in the Stott family that the first words John ever spoke were 'coronary thrombosis'. We will never know if that's true.

Fascinating Fact 2

HARLEY STREET

Harley Street, built in the reign of Queen Victoria, soon became the best address in the world for medical consultants, like John's father. One end is just a few minutes' walk from Regents Park and the other end close to the Oxford Street shops. The film *The King's Speech* made 146 Harley Street famous. It was the house King George VI visited often, to have his stammer cured.

The architect of this area of London was John Nash, one of the most famous of his day. Lilias Trotter, the pioneer missionary to North Africa, grew up in Devonshire Place House, a few minutes' walk away; Sherlock Holmes, the fictional detective, had his office about ten minutes' walk to the west, at 221B Baker Street, close to Madame Tussaud's; and Samuel Morse, who invented the Morse code, lived nearby for a while, at 141 Cleveland Street.

Chapter 2

Off to School
(1927-1940)

'Joanna did well at King Arthur's' said Lily, as she and Arnold discussed a school for Joy. 'Yes, she did do well there,' agreed Arnold. King Arthur's School in Kensington seemed a good choice for Joy – it was fairly small, easy to get to, and the staff cared about the children.

Education was important to the Stotts, and they wanted the best for each of their children. Joanna had moved on to boarding school before Joy arrived at King Arthur's.

The Stotts had the same conversation about John, two years later. (He was first taught at home by a governess.) Aged six, he joined Joy at King Arthur's, wearing his slightly-too-big school blazer, and with his cap pressed down firmly over his new haircut. His governess had already taught him how to write, and he was good at drawing. He especially enjoyed drawing birds and all his life he kept two drawings from those days. One was of a parrot, carefully coloured in, using his brightest pencils; and the other of an owl. He loved to write about birds too. The walks in Regent's Park with his father sparked an interest in the natural world which never left him.

Joy took him to his classroom. 'This is my brother,' she said shyly, handing him over to his teacher. 'Ah, another Stott', said John's teacher. Some staff at King Arthur's remembered Joanna, too. Doubtless comparisons were made, as teachers always make comparisons.

John's mother had encouraged him in learning a little French at home. Many children learn numbers in a new language, so they can count up to ten or even twenty before their formal lessons begin. This introduction to a language is always a help, and builds confidence.

But when the class launched into French, and a few proudly demonstrated their 'un, deux, trois…' John was clearly ahead of the game. He could write about his favourite animal in French. John didn't just *love* animals. He found out what they ate, how they built their homes, how they related to their young. Like many children, he was drawn to elephants. By the age of seven, he had already composed this French riddle:

DEVINETTE	*Riddle*
Devinez qui je suis	*Guess who I am*
Etes-vous un animal?	*Are you an animal?*
Oui, je suis un animal	*Yes, I am an animal*
Avez-vous quatre pattes?	*Do you have four paws?*
Oui, j'ai quatre pattes	*Yes, I have four paws*
Etes-vous grand?	*Are you big?*
Oui, je suis grand	*Yes, I am big*
Habitez-vous le Zoo?	*Do you live in the Zoo?*
Oui, j'habite le Zoo	*Yes, I live in the Zoo*
Mangez-vous du foin?	*Do you eat hay?*
Oui, je mange du foin	*Yes, I eat hay*
Aimez-vous les gâteaux?	*Do you like cakes?*
Oui, j'aime bien les gâteaux	*Yes, I love cakes*
Avez-vous une trompe?	*Do you have a trunk?*
Oui, j'ai une trompe	*Yes, I have a trunk*
Etes-vous un elephant?	*Are you an elephant?*
Oui, je suis un elephant	*Yes, I am an elephant*

John enjoyed King Arthur's School, and the car journey there and back each day with Joy. But two years later, changes were in store. When he was eight, and just a few weeks after he was rebuked for 'unruly behaviour' in the park, he was to leave home. His parents were sending him to boarding school. They chose Oakley Hall, in Cirencester, about a hundred miles away.

Joanna was always full of stories when she came home from boarding school. It sounded fun. So when John heard this news, he got quite excited. Everything seemed to happen quickly, and over the next few weeks he was fitted out with his new uniform, towels, sheets, pyjamas, sports gear… and the whole school list.

'You can choose what else to take with you,' said his Nanny, helping him to pack. He chose some of his favourite books, his toy guns and daggers, his roller skates, and his butterfly net.

Oakley Hall

'Please be extra careful with my butterfly net,' John said politely to his father's chauffeur. John had started to build a fine collection of butterflies, so his butterfly net had to go with him to Oakley Hall. The school trunk and tuck box of goodies had been loaded into the family Chrysler, each bearing the initials JRWS carefully stencilled on the top. The chauffeur now laid John's precious butterfly net on top of everything else. The car was ready to leave, and after a three-hour drive a new stage of life was about to begin.

'This is your bed over here,' Matron told him. 'I'll help you unpack.'

John found he would sleep in a dormitory with seven or eight others. There were strict rules about lights out, and when to stop talking, but new boys soon got used to everything, though they missed home. In winter the dorms got very cold, as there was no central heating then. In the morning it was sometimes so cold that the water in the wash basins, poured ready for the boys to wash, had ice forming on its surface.

At Oakley Hall John learned a good deal of British history, largely through the stories of battles, and he could recite the dates of the reigns of kings and queens.

Classroom teaching in those days was based around a lot of reciting, and the children began by reciting their multiplication tables. The whole class would chant together to a rhythm never forgotten.
    One two is two (which seemed rather obvious to John)
    two twos are four
    three twos are six

four twos are eight
five twos are ten
and so forth. All tables up to the twelve times table were covered in this way.

French verbs were recited by the class out loud too. John had begun to recite French verbs at King Arthur's, so he was comfortably ahead in this at Oakley Hall. The first French verb most children learn is *porter* (to wear or carry), to show how 'er' verbs behave. Then they learn *venir* (to come), to show how the 'ir' verbs behave. John knew both, and, as we saw in the riddle, he had also mastered *être* and *avoir* (to be and to have).

John's Scripture teacher found he could recall several stories from the Old and New Testaments. Something must have lodged from the All Souls Sunday School lessons before he was sent out of the room! Altogether he was doing well.

'What do you make of John Stott?' asked one of the younger teachers in the staff room one day. He didn't teach John, and wondered what he was like in the classroom. John was evidently bright, and he was also full of pranks. How did teachers manage to contain his lively spirit when the whole class had to slog through irregular French verbs? Especially if he knew them already!

'Likeable rogue,' came the reply from behind a newspaper. This expression, used by older teachers, was a kind of shorthand. It stood for: 'Yes, they misbehave, and it can disturb the class. But it shows they've got something about them.' That 'something' is often leadership in the making. John was one of the brightest in the class, and he almost always smiled; it would have been hard *not* to like him, but that did not stop him from being beaten with a cane. He was caned at least three times in his first year. He wrote to his parents about the canings in letters home, adding in all honesty, 'I don't know why I keep being caned!'

John could hold his own at cricket and he played for the school Second XI at soccer. He was good at acting, and had a fine singing voice. So with the happy combination of natural talent and of getting into trouble from time to time, he became a popular boy.

If French came easily to John, Latin was harder. This was partly because at first he couldn't sort out the 'subject' of a sentence from the 'object' of a sentence. In Latin this matters a lot. The same word can have a different ending, depending on whether it is subject or object. For some nouns the ending for both is identical. But for the first group of nouns the children were taught (called 'the first declension') the ending is different. John didn't want to lose marks. Neither did he want his teacher to think he was stupid. So like all intelligent schoolboys, he found a way around the problem which worked brilliantly, at least for the first declension. In Latin the word for table is 'mens*a*' when it is the subject of a sentence, and 'mens*am*' when it is the object. So what was his ruse?

'I would write "mensam" if I wasn't sure, and then put a faint pencil line through the "m". If it should have been "mensa" the teacher would think the final letter had been crossed out. But if "mensam" was right, the teacher would see the line, but as it was faint, would just ignore it.' A shrewd plan!

A disaster in the nursery

In school holidays, John continued to go with his father on nature walks. As well as teaching John to observe, his father also taught him the names of plants, and of butterflies and birds. Arnold explained to John what we call the eco-system; that is how plants and animals, birds and insects all depend on one another. These nature walks led to John's earliest hobby of collecting butterflies.

One day his father handed him a glass bottle with a tight lid.

    Arnold Johnnie, promise me you will be careful with this.

    John What's it for, Daddy?

    Arnold It's a killing bottle. It will kill butterflies instantly. Then you can add them to your collection. But you need to promise me you won't sniff it.

    John I promise.

John realized only years later that if he had sniffed it, it could have killed *him* as well as the butterflies, as it contained cyanide! John's father evidently had a high level of trust in his son.

In the summer holiday, John and his father would go 'sugaring' in the evenings, to catch butterflies and moths. They laid traps, mixing beer and treacle, and then at night his father would wake him and they would go out together to see what was caught. Inebriated by the beer, hapless butterflies and moths would lie on the ground, ready for John to examine. John left the more common ones to fly off again the next day, and placed the rarer ones in his killing bottle, to add to his collection. Over time John amassed a collection to be proud of. He may have had dreams of becoming a world expert on butterflies. But during one school holiday, disaster struck.

In the nursery one day, when John was carefully setting new butterflies in the display, Joy threw a cushion at him. It landed right in the centre of the butterfly box and destroyed it in an instant.

'Joy, look what you've *done*!' He was stunned. All his work had been ruined. The care and love in mounting the specimens was now worth nothing.

Joy was silent, then started to cry loudly, and Nanny rushed in to see what was happening. Joy was as upset as John was. The butterfly collection meant everything to him. His father knew that, and tried to repair it, but it was beyond repair. John was devastated.

Many years later, John Stott spoke about the incident. 'I had probably provoked Joy,' he said. 'So it was partly my own fault.' Then he added, 'It was then that I turned to birds, and I have often used this as a good parable of the Providence of God. I was inconsolable at the time, of course, but I'm very glad now.'

John Stott became an expert on birds from every continent. He said with a grin: 'People think one is eccentric enough to go around the world with binoculars. To have gone around the world with a butterfly net would have been much too much to bear.'

The family often spent summers out of London. Some time after the butterfly incident, when John was nine years old, and the Stotts were on holiday, his father gave him a gift he prized dearly. It was a book, beautifully-bound, and inscribed in the front:

Johnnie
  from Daddy
19th August 1930
Burton Bradstock, Dorset

John knew straight away what he wanted to do with it. In his best handwriting on the flyleaf he inscribed the words: **Nature Notebook**

Turning over to the first page and with great care, he wrote at the top: *List of Birds Seen* then he began to list them, and the list grew:
  Crow
  Rook
  Blackbird
  Robin
  Thrush
  Kingfisher
  Green Woodpecker
  Cormorant

The book went back with him to boarding school. It became a constant companion. In school holidays he would roller-skate up to Regents Park on his own, and see what he could find. Over the next nine years he filled 150 pages, closely-lined. The pages included the names of birds, descriptions of where and when he observed them, and some short essays on their behaviour and their habitats.

The following year, a teacher called Robbie Bickersteth arrived to teach at Oakley Hall. Mr Bickersteth, like John's father, was keen on nature, and he soon became a friend of the whole family.

'Write to me, John. Tell me what new birds you and your Daddy see,' Robbie Bickersteth would say, at the end of term. He and John would occasionally go on bird-watching expeditions in the north of England and in Scotland during the school holidays. John always took his precious ledger with him.

John and Robbie kept in touch all through John's schooldays and while he was a student. There was no social media in those days, nor email; and no-one had a mobile phone. John's family and Robbie both had landlines, but in those days people used them sparingly as long-distance phone calls were expensive. So the best way to keep in touch was by writing letters. John and Robbie wrote often to each other throughout John's schooldays, and shared their thoughts on many things. John admired Robbie a great deal.

Final year at Oakley Hall

All too soon John was in his final year at Oakley Hall. It was a year with some big surprises. The first came when he was called into the headmaster's office soon after he had unpacked and once again put his school trunk into the store. Wondering what he had done wrong, he straightened his tie, and knocked on the headmaster's door. The headmaster's reason for summoning him was to tell him he was being made head boy!

Then John received more good news. He was chosen to play the part of Mark Antony in the school play, Shakespeare's *Julius Caesar*. He received fine reviews for his 'Friends, Romans, Countrymen' speech.

John knew how badly his parents wanted him to go to Rugby School. He worked as hard as he could before the entrance exam, and it was a relief to have it behind him. Then, like all the boys sitting this exam, he sat nervously, waiting for the results. His parents would be so disappointed if he didn't get a place.

'Do you know when the results will come, Sir?' John asked his form teacher.

'I'm as keen as you to hear,' came the reply. 'You've worked hard, and I know you'll have done your best. I think you'll be fine.'

After a few tense days, the news arrived. It came by telegram from his parents.

> 23 NOVEMBER 1934:
> HEARTIEST CONGRATULATIONS ON GETTING AMONG THE FIRST THREE
> LOVE MUMMY AND DADDY

So the following year John went up to Rugby School, the birthplace of rugby football.

Rugby School

'I'd like John to be in Kilbracken, my old house, if possible,' wrote Arnold Stott to the school registrar. Kilbracken was then sited at 1 Hillmorton Road, a large redbrick building, housing around 80 boys. It wasn't very comfortable, some called it spartan. The registrar placed John's name on the Kilbracken list. (This school house was relocated to a better building shortly after John left.)

A pattern continued as John travelled to and from Rugby. At the beginning of each term, Dr Stott's chauffeur would fill the Chrysler with petrol, and then pack it. This done, he would park it by the front door of number 58 Harley Street.

Chauffeur The car's outside now, Master John.

John Thank you. I'm almost ready.

First John had to say his goodbyes.

The journey from London to Rugby took much longer than it would now. Rugby is just five miles from Junction 15 of the M1. But the M1 was not opened until 1959. So John's journey began up the A1 from London, known as the Great North Road. Eventually signs appeared for The Midlands, and then for the town of Rugby. Life in Kilbracken was once more in sight.

John enjoyed being at Rugby. As with all new schools, he had to settle in, find his way around, learn the subculture, and make new friends. He played the cello, and sang in the choir; he acted in the school plays; he ran regularly for the school in cross-country events. Each day was full, with activities crammed around his work. His full and varied schedule meant he quickly got to know a lot of boys from other houses. He was friendly, and took an interest in other people, so he would naturally fall into conversation as he walked from Kilbracken to chapel, then on to classes, or to the library.

John would point out birds to his friends as they walked between school buildings. 'Look!' he would interject mid-sentence. 'Did you see that?' Then he would stand completely still, craning his ear to hear birdsong. His friends laughed at his passion and dedication. Maybe years later they were saying to their own children, 'There was a boy at Rugby called Stott who told us to shut our mouths and open our eyes and ears. We laughed at him. But you know, we learned a lot when we did it.'

While school uniform was a sports jacket, a few boys wore blazers. These boys were members of the Levée. The Levée was a Rugby tradition (and it still is). It met regularly to help govern the school, and to shape school policy. This committee was made up of heads of houses, with two extra places only. When John entered the sixth form, aged 17, he learned that the Levée had given him one of these places. He wrote to his parents with great excitement, and asked if he might order a blazer from the school shop. The reply came almost immediately. His father had not been on the Levée while he was at Rugby. He could not have been more proud of his son.

John was a natural leader. He became chairman of the Levée, head of Kilbracken House, and then head boy of the school. John gave disciplined time to each responsibility, as well as to his studies. (Every school speech day saw him walk across the platform to collect prizes.) In his final year he even found time to take the title role in the school play, Shakespeare's *Richard II*.

But as John Stott looked back on his schooldays in later life, it was not these achievements which stood out for him. It was something quite different. A Sunday afternoon meeting would change everything about the way he thought. It was to change *everything*, full stop.

An afternoon which changed John's life

John Bridger, a friend in the year above, and a member of the Levée, ran a Christian Union meeting after lunch on Sundays, and John Stott had been along to it once or twice. One day early in February 1938, not long before John's seventeenth birthday, John Bridger was walking over to the library with him. John Bridger was good at everything. He played cricket, hockey and rugby for the school's first teams, and, like John, was outstanding in modern languages. He had become a Christian two years earlier. John Stott admired John Bridger.

John Bridger John, a friend of mine will be here on Sunday to speak at the meeting. I think you'd like him. Are you free to come?

John Stott Well, I have nothing in my schedule for that time. All right. Yes, I'll come.

John Bridger had been praying for John Stott for several months. But how would John respond to what he heard at the meeting? John Bridger knew that was up to God, and not up to him. He prayed that his friend would indeed come, and not change his mind, and that he would listen carefully.

That Sunday, John Stott walked into the classroom in New Quad in good time for the start of the meeting, and sat down. John had been aware of his need for God, but had not found him. He had read his Bible, as he promised his mother he would, and sometimes he crept into the school chapel by himself, to read religious books, and absorb what he described as 'the atmosphere of mystery'. He wanted to know God for himself, but was unable to get beyond his searching. He envied John Bridger for his clear and confident faith.

The speaker that afternoon was a man called Eric Nash (better known by his nickname Bash). John found himself listening intently. Bash explained that the boys needed to *do* something with Christ. They could not just remain neutral about him. 'Either you reject him, or you follow him,' said Bash.

John had been baptized as an infant, and confirmed in the chapel at Rugby eighteen months earlier; he had read his Bible and said his prayers. But he was very conscious that he did not know Christ. A new longing in his heart was stirred. So at the end of the meeting he introduced himself to the speaker.

John There are some questions I'd like to ask you, if I may, sir.

Bash Do call me Bash, please. Everyone does. And yes, I'd love to hear your questions. Let's go for a drive. It will give us time to talk.

Here was an able boy with a genuine desire to speak about spiritual matters. Bash wanted to avoid any interruptions, so he could give John his full attention.

'My car's just over there,' he said, as they walked around the corner of the building. They headed out of town and for the next two hours they talked deeply. John told Bash all about himself, and Bash listened. Bash never put pressure on people, and he put no pressure on John that afternoon. He explained that everyone is born with sin in their hearts, and that this sin separates us from God. He then showed John how we can become friends of God, how we can know him, through his Son, Jesus Christ. This is what John needed to hear. That afternoon he was more aware than ever of his desire to know God. Bash found a place to park, then he pulled out his New Testament which he carried with him everywhere. Opening it at John's gospel, he handed it to John.

> **Bash** Here, John, see what your namesake the Apostle John wrote. Look at John's gospel chapter 3 and verse 16. This is like a summary of why Jesus died. Read it.
>
> **John** For God so loved the world that he gave his one and only Son that whoever believes in him will not perish but have eternal life.

Then Bash flicked over the pages.

> **Bash** And here's what the Apostle John wrote years later. Jesus gave him a special vision which he wrote down. It's all in the last book of the Bible, called Revelation. In the vision he receives a message for each of the churches in Asia. I just want to show you one verse.

John was intrigued.

> **Bash** It's in the message to the church in Laodicea. Here, take a look at chapter 3, verse 20. Don't worry if you've never heard of Laodicea before. It's Jesus speaking to that church, but it's also Jesus speaking to *you*, right now.

Bash once more pointed to the place for John to read:

> **John** *[reading]* Here I am! I stand at the door and knock. If anyone hears my voice and opens the door, I will come in and eat with him, and he with me.

It was already dark by the time Bash dropped John outside Kilbracken. That evening when John prayed, God was no longer shrouded in mystery. Now he knew for sure what he needed to *do* with Christ. He resolved to follow him for the rest of his life.

John wrote in his diary two days later, on Tuesday, 15 February 1938:

> I really have felt an immense and new joy throughout today. It is the joy of being at peace with the world, - and of being in touch with God. How well do I know that He rules me, - and that I never really knew Him before.

Bash visited Rugby regularly, and spent time with John, helping him build a daily habit of reading and praying. Bash also prayed for John. Not long after their first meeting, Bash gave him a small New Testament. On the flyleaf he inscribed the words:

> **I can do all things through Christ who strengthens me.**
> **Philippians 4:13**
> E.J.H.N.

Bash wrote a letter to John every single week for the next five years. In these letters, Bash outlined major doctrines of the Christian faith, or raised ethical issues he wanted John to think through, or he gave advice on how to help younger boys who had become Christians. Sometimes he rebuked John, if he sensed that was needed. Bash's letters could be very weighty, but they always ended with a joke, to keep John from being too serious!

Bash ran an Easter camp and a summer camp for boys from the top public schools, including Rugby. John Bridger went to these camps. The summer camp was held in Dorset. John was there in 1938 and he loved it. The camp officers (leaders) taught the boys the basic truths of the Christian faith, while also teaching them leadership skills. John went back the following year, this time as a camp officer. Bash thought the best way for John to learn to lead was to throw him in at the deep end.

Jesus invested time in a small group of disciples for his three years of public ministry. People like Bash sought to follow that model. We can't invest in many people, as time would be spread too thinly. Bash could see in John a gift of leadership which would one day tower high above his own. (Recognizing this in a younger person is a mark of humility.) As he prepared for the summer camp of 1940, Bash had a new idea, which involved John. He explained it the next time they met.

Bash John, I want you to become Camp Secretary.

John was very honoured, but also surprised. He was still at school and there were several older officers who could do it better. He wanted to be sure he could manage the role well, and his days were already very full.

John What will that mean?

> **Bash** Food is always important. Let's start there. You would need to order the food, and make sure we have a team of cooks. Check with those who came last year and see if they can come again.

John was writing things down.

> **John** Yes, I could do that.

He looked up again, and he could tell from Bash's face that Bash hadn't finished.

> **Bash** There's something more. We need to help the war effort.

The Second World War had begun in 1939, and it affected the whole nation.

> **Bash** I think we should give time each day to helping local farmers. Or doing other practical work in the area. I know it's a lot to ask, but I'd need you to get in touch with farmers in the area, and find out what we can do.

John gulped a little. He could see the time needed for letters, phone calls, more letters. But he knew Bash could not easily manage this, as he was travelling around the country to visit boys in school.

> **John** Let me think and pray about it. Could you give me a few days to do that?

Bash agreed. He was glad to see this measure of maturity in the way John made decisions. John wrote to Bash with his decision the following week. He took on the role.

In his heart, John seriously began to wonder if God may be leading him to serve as an ordained minister in the Anglican church. He knew his father had high hopes for him, perhaps in the Diplomatic Service. John's sharp mind, peace-loving spirit and excellence in language skills would have suited him so well for this. How would the idea of becoming a rector of a church be received? John Stott's father was a life-long agnostic, and the thought of his only son doing this seemed like a waste of a good brain and a good education.

Fascinating Fact 3

RUGBY SCHOOL

Rugby School was founded in 1567. The boys wear sports jackets, and the girls (first admitted to the school in the 1970s) wear similar jackets with long skirts, reaching their ankles. Some girls wear their pyjamas underneath their skirts in winter! Pedometers, unknown in John's day, can now be worn for fun. On a school day, pupils can easily cover at least five miles, walking between their house, and the classrooms, specialist rooms like IT, science blocks, and chapel.

Many Old Rugbeians have become famous. For example Lewis Carroll who wrote *Alice in Wonderland*, Arthur Ransome who wrote *Swallows and Amazons,* and Rupert Brooke, the First World War poet. Today tourists can buy rugby balls in the school shop. The game was invented by a pupil, William Webb-Ellis. He didn't set out to invent a new game; he simply disregarded the rules while playing football one afternoon. On what became an historic day in 1823, he grabbed the ball and ran with it. The opposing team called for him to be sent off. But some people wondered if rules should instead be changed. Should it be allowed, or shouldn't it? This became a serious discussion in the school, and in sporting circles. Within ten years, the novel way of playing became a new game in itself. The game was named rugby after the school where it began.

Fascinating Fact 4

TWO RUGBY HEADMASTERS

Dr Thomas Arnold (father of the poet Matthew Arnold) served as headmaster of Rugby School from 1828 to 1842, and brought many changes. He is regarded as the school's greatest headmaster. *Tom Brown's Schooldays* - set in Dr Arnold's time - was translated into French in the 1870s, and made a deep impact on Pierre de Coubertin, who later founded the modern Olympic Games. Pierre de Coubertin visited Rugby, and said Dr Arnold was a profound influence on his life and thought.

While John was a pupil, Percival Hugh Lyon was the headmaster. John liked Hugh Lyon and got to know him better than most pupils did, as he served as head of house and then head boy of the school. Dr Lyon was a man with a strong and positive spirit, and he wrote poetry. He had previously been Rector of Edinburgh Academy. There is a plaque to his memory in the school chapel.

Fascinating Fact 5

A NEW HOUSE AND A NEW HONOUR

When John was aged 15, the family moved across the road to number 65 Harley Street. It was larger, so his father's consulting rooms and the family quarters could be kept separate.

In the evenings the family would change for dinner. John and his father wore dinner jackets and Joy and his mother evening gowns. (By this stage Joanna had left home.) When dinner was over, John and Joy would sometimes roll back the carpet in the great drawing room, and dance to gramophone records.

That same year, in 1936, Dr Stott gained a special honour. He received a letter from Buckingham Palace inviting him to become a Physician to the Royal Household. John was at school when the news broke, and he sent his father a telegram:

HEARTIEST CONGRATULATIONS SIMPLY GRAND BRAVO JOHN

Telegrams were the fastest and surest way of getting news to a person, hand-delivered by a boy on a bicycle. They were always written in capital letters, with the words stuck onto the sheet of paper. There was no punctuation, so a full stop would be written as 'STOP'. The message was then folded into an envelope and sealed. Telegrams were kept short, as their cost was based on the number of words. STOP counted as a word, which is why it was sometimes left out.

CHAPTER 3
A STUDENT AT CAMBRIDGE (1940-1944)

A few weeks after camp, John entered Cambridge University to read French and German.

The university is now made up of over 30 independent colleges, scattered around the town. John had applied to Trinity College, where his father and Bash had both studied, one of the largest colleges in the university. Most colleges are designed around quadrangles, with buildings around the sides, overlooking a striped lawn. In Oxford University these are called quads after their shape, but in Cambridge University they are called courts. Trinity Great Court is one of the most striking quadrangles in the world.

'Welcome to Trinity! I'm Oliver Barclay.' A third year student at Trinity introduced himself to John, and they shook hands. 'I live over there,' Oliver said, pointing to his room. 'Drop in for tea today, if you have time. Say 3.30?'

John and Oliver became good friends from that afternoon. Oliver was studying zoology. He was from a Quaker background, and the Quakers were conscientious objectors – or pacifists, so Oliver had been excused military service. John had also been excused military service, as he believed it was morally wrong for Christians to go to war. John and Oliver shared a deep desire to serve God, and to get to know the Bible better. They spent much time together in discussion, walking round and round Trinity Great Court, or along the Backs of the colleges, 'trying to solve all the problems of church and state'. Some friendships built in student years can last for life; the friendship between John and Oliver was one of those.

Before John went up to Cambridge, his father urged him not to join the Christian Union in the university, as he did not think it would be good for John. John wanted to honour his father, so he promised he would not join, and he kept his promise. The Cambridge Inter-Collegiate Christian Union (CICCU) is still very active today, with a group in each of the colleges. Oliver was a member. While John never formally joined, he did play a full and enthusiastic role in both the Trinity group and the central meetings.

Bash's letters continued to arrive, week by week. Bash had been impressed by John's work as Camp Secretary. He was more than a good Secretary. He took his own spiritual growth seriously, and it showed in his attitudes, his work and his friendships.

As Bash began to cast his mind into the future, he wondered who should follow him. The camp work largely depended on Bash. What if he should be taken ill, or die unexpectedly? He had excellent young camp officers – church leaders, schoolteachers and school chaplains. They were all committed to the camps work. Should he approach one of them, and ask if they would step into his shoes if the need arose? Which one should he ask? As he reflected prayerfully on this matter, it was to John he looked.

When John was still in his first year at Cambridge, a month before his 20th birthday, Bash composed the following note on his letterhead:

> From The Rev E. J. H. NASH,
> 10 Craufurd Rise, Maidenhead, Phone 1034

> If anything should happen to me, I wish that John Stott shall assume full and absolute control of Kippers – Beachborough – Iwerne Minster Camp. He knows my mind and will guide and appoint officers as he sees fit.
> E. J. H. Nash
> 30 March 1941

Bash lived many more years, but a note like this illustrates the stature shown by John Stott as a young man.

'John, I'd love to see you take over the schools work when you graduate,' Bash wrote to him. 'You excel as Camp Secretary, and I know you would be well-respected by masters and boys alike in the schools.'

'I hope I never lose contact with camp,' John replied. 'I'm grateful for your confidence in me, Bash. I've been praying about my future, as I know you have, but I don't think the schools work is for me. I sense I may be called into the Anglican church.'

Bash trusted John's judgment in this as in other areas. John went on reassuringly, 'I am committed to the twin authorities of the Bible and the Person of Jesus Christ. Committed to them above everything else.'

As modern languages finals drew close in the summer of 1942, John applied to begin studying theology the following year. He was determined to do well in modern languages, and he did. He was awarded first class honours in French.

He gained first class honours in theology, too. In 1944 he changed college to Ridley Hall, to train for the church.

Fascinating Fact 6

EARLY TO BED AND EARLY TO RISE

Uncle John was a gifted administrator, a spiritual leader, very intelligent and highly self-disciplined in his use of time. To achieve a good degree, and do other things alongside, meant strict self-discipline. He would get up at 6.00am to give himself an hour and a half of quiet – first to read the Bible and pray, and then to read *The Times*, before arriving for breakfast in Hall (the college dining room) at 8.00am. He would return to Hall for lunch at 12.55pm, and be back at his desk by 1.45pm.

Early rising was a habit for life. In due course he would get up even earlier, and then take a 'horizontal half hour' or 'HHH' after lunch to rest each day. It is not easy to get up early on dark, cold wintry mornings. As a student, John found that the secret to early rising is going to bed on time.

'It was always the same,' said his friend at Cambridge, John Sheldon, 'even when discussion was in full flow. As soon as the college clock struck 9.30, John would leave. He got up early, and it was the only way to do it.'

Chapter 4
Pacifism and War

John's letters to his family while a student

Now we take a close-up view on a wartime issue – pacifism. This would leave a deep mark on John Stott's relationship with his family.

Many boys in John's school year joined the armed forces, and then went on to university after the Second World War finished. In the normal course of events, John would have done the same, perhaps becoming a soldier, or joining the Navy or the Royal Air Force. But he did not want to do this as he was a pacifist. His father became a major general in the medical corps, and found John's pacifism very hard to cope with.

Arnold Stott felt it was John's *duty* to serve the nation by joining the forces. But John could not go against his conscience. The difficult relationship with his father over this time was painful to him, and he wrote long and careful letters to his parents, from school, and then from Cambridge, to try to help them understand.

John's father resolved not to pay for John's university expenses after his first year, if he would not join up. This was a huge blow to John for there were no student loans then. But still John felt he could not go against his conscience. His mother broke the news to John about his fees in a letter, soon after the beginning of the Lent Term, in January 1941. He scribbled a note in the margin of the letter:

>   The order is not State 1st, Jesus 2nd
>   but Jesus 1st, State 2nd.

I must obey God rather than men
ACTS 5:29

John wrote back affectionately to his mother, to say he would think about things further and would like to talk again with his father. He wanted to reassure her that he was not seeking his own comfort in staying at university during the war, but that he honestly believed this was his duty. He signed the letter;

Always your loving son

His mother wrote often, and tried hard to persuade John to change his mind, but he felt unable to do so. With care always to express his honour for his parents, and his deep affection for his family, John carefully outlined his reasons. The draft remains of one letter in John's small handwriting, which ran to nine sides. He yearned that his father would come to understand. Arnold Stott came to Cambridge to meet with John's tutor, and it was agreed that John would talk with senior churchmen in the town, which he willingly did.

Lily Stott felt caught in the middle. Over this period, she wrote to her son every few days, addressing him fondly as Johnnie, and sometimes Johntie or Jonathan. She believed in her heart that John's father was right, and that John should join up, for non-combatant duties if he preferred. She longed for him to change his mind, or for Arnold to relent. It was a heart-rending time for all three of them.

John's end-of-year exams began on 2nd June. They counted towards his final degree, so he wanted to do well. He kept on working hard, playing some sport, participating in the CICCU, and squeezing in some birdwatching with Oliver or other friends where possible. One can imagine his heavy heart, and the stress of the money issue always on his mind. Then on 19th May, three weeks before his exams began, there was a knock on his door and he was handed a telegram.

John quickly slit open the envelope and pulled out the paper. He had received a telegram from his parents when he won the place at Rugby. Here was another which marked a life-changing moment, and he could barely believe what he saw. His prayers, and the prayers of his friends, had been answered in a wonderful way. The telegram read:

AM CONSENTING STOP BUT WITH GREAT RELUCTANCE
AND UNHAPPINESS STOP STOTT

John would now be staying at Cambridge. With thankfulness to God in his heart, he raced around to share the news.

He wanted his father to be proud of him, in the best sense of taking pride in one's children. His father was proud of Joanna and Joy for their contributions to the war. If only he could be glad that John was making best use of all his parents had given him – a sharp intellect, a sense of loyalty to his family and to his nation, and much delight in the natural world. John knew there was a lot of work to be done to restore their relationship.

The Stotts had been a warm, affectionate family, and now things were so different. John's mother and his sisters all felt the same, that he had made a big mistake.

Fascinating Fact 7

SEEING THINGS DIFFERENTLY

In years to come, John Stott realized that not all Christians are pacifists. It surprised him at first. No-one explained to him that there could be a 'just war' in which it was right for Christians to take part. Had this been explained, he felt he would have changed his position. Nearly fifty years later, Oliver Barclay edited a book on Pacifism and War in a series called *When Christians Disagree*. He too had come to see that the matter was not as clear-cut as he first thought.

Photo captions

1. John and Joy with Nanny Golden
2. On John's fourth birthday
3. Cricket on the beach
4. With Joy in Park Square Gardens
5. Capturing a photo of the Snowy Owl after a long search
6. Young sportsman at Oakley Hall, probably 1928
7. Sports Day at Oakley Hall, 1929
8. Off to school in the family Chrysler, 1931
9. Schoolboy at Oakley Hall
10. Rugby School
11. Oakley Hall football team (John is on the captain's left)
12. All Souls Church in 1940
13. Robbie Bickersteth, schoolmaster and friend
14. Birdwatching in Suffolk with a friend
15. Joy, Joanna and John Stott
16. As Camp Secretary, with Bash
17. As Richard lll in the school play, 1939
18. 'Played 24. Won 24'. Late 1940s

11

12

13

Chapter 5

Training for the Church at Ridley Hall (1944-45)

Cambridge is small, so nowhere is more than a few minutes on a bike from anywhere else.

Ridley Hall is a Victorian redbrick building, named after Nicholas Ridley, a Reformation martyr, who was burned to death for his faith in 1555.

John had a room on Staircase E. Other names painted alongside his at the entrance to that staircase were those of three good friends: John Bridger and Philip Tompson from Rugby days, and John Sheldon, his friend at Trinity.

'Are you coming to the lecture this morning? Philip Tompson asked.

'No, I think I'll go the library,' John would answer. It was the same most mornings.

John used his time at Ridley more for personal study than for lectures. He read books written by the lecturers, and he read more widely, too. This seemed a more productive way of spending his time. And his time was always tight. Off he would stride to the library, taking a shortcut through Clare Memorial Court, with his gown flowing behind him. 'You could set your watch by him,' said John Collins, then a student at Clare.

Map of Cambridge

Showing just a few buildings from this story. There are over 30 University colleges in this small medieaval town.

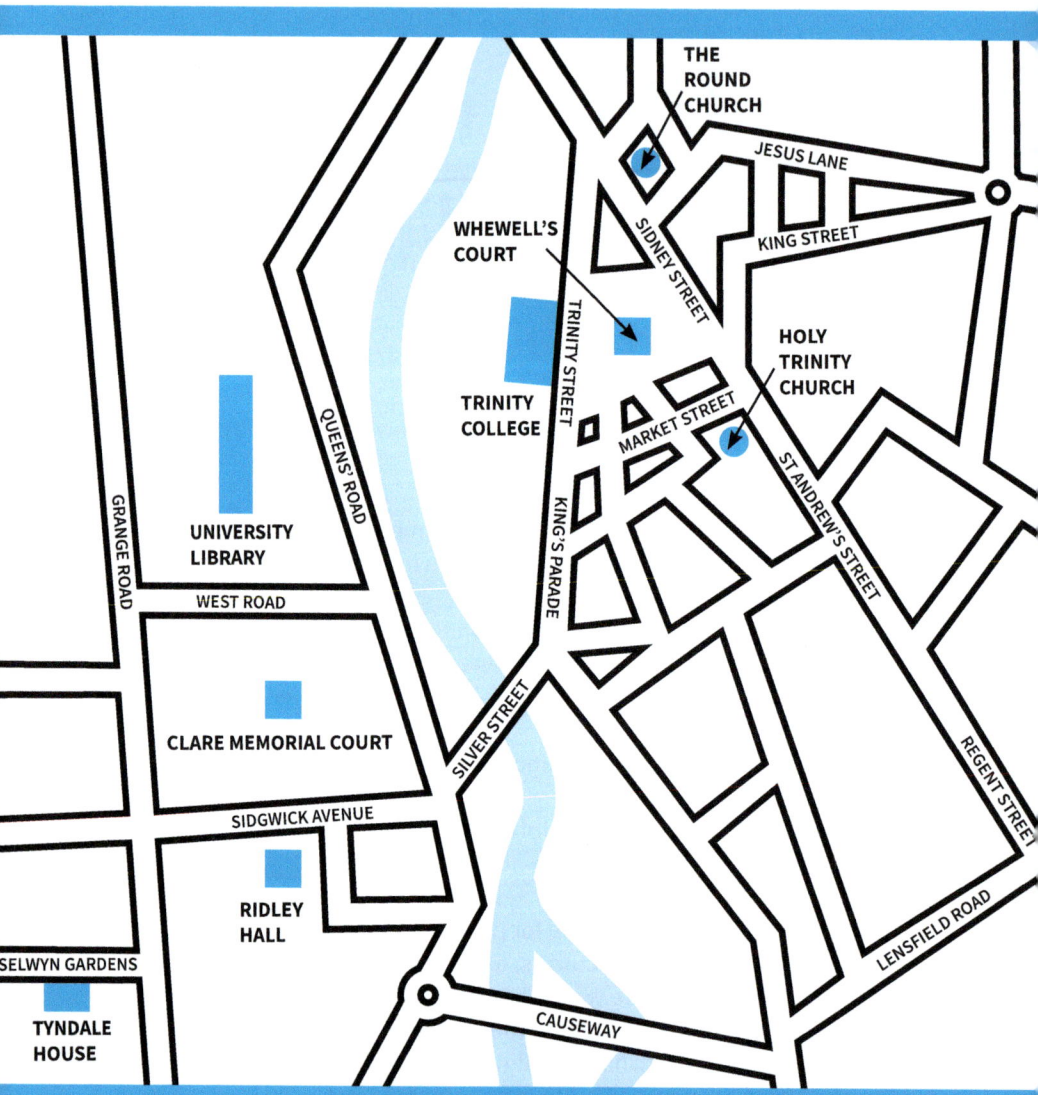

Map is not to scale

John Stott was often invited to college Christian Union groups, speaking to as many as four colleges per week. John would sometimes take his bike with him to the library, or walk back through Clare Mem Court and grab his bike at Ridley. Either way, he could be at a college group within a few minutes.

John started speaking to college CU groups while he was at Trinity. At one stage the Girton College Christian Union wanted him to speak. One of its members cycled down to Trinity to invite him. She propped her bicycle against the wall of Whewell's Court, and looked for his name. Then she climbed the dark staircase, and was about to knock on the big oak door of his rooms when she caught sight of a typewritten notice. It read:

Working 8am – 8pm. Please do not disturb unless absolutely necessary.

She crept back down the stairs again, and cycled off. In those days she couldn't text him, or Whatsapp him. She could have left a note in his pigeonhole in the Porters' Lodge if she had thought of it. But the notice left her too stunned to think of it, and so he was not invited to Girton after all!

That student was Myra Chave-Jones. She would often see John in the University Library. 'He worked with iron self-discipline,' she said. 'He would enter silently, go to his usual corner, reach for books, and settle down with total concentration.' Myra became a good friend of John Stott years later, and they laughed about the notice on his door.

Several Ridley men had been greatly helped in their faith through the CICCU. On Sunday evenings the CICCU held a weekly evangelistic address in Holy Trinity Church, for members to invite their friends. John Stott, John Sheldon, Philip Tompson and John Bridger were there every week. They helped with stewarding, and were often asked to talk with younger students who wanted to know more about the Christian faith. They sat down with students in the same way Bash had sat down with each of them.

While at Ridley Hall, John received a letter inviting him to write an article for the national Scripture Union magazine. It was his first article for a national magazine. He mentioned it to Philip Tompson that day over lunch

Philip What's it on?

John The importance of teaching the Christian faith to children.

> **Philip** Hmmmm… [digging into his wartime spam, a rather pink meat substitute, as enthusiastically as he could] Didn't you just speak about that to a group planning a beach mission?
>
> **John** I did. Thank you for remembering. Aren't these beach missions wonderful for teaching Bible stories to children! People can write children off as too young to understand their need of Christ. But we need to teach them what sin means. And it's dangerous to be shallow, just because they're young.
>
> **Philip** More water?

Philip filled their glasses as John paused to eat, before he continued.

> **John** They have their whole lives ahead of them – to live for God, and to speak of him.

As John began writing his article, he drew illustrations from the prophet Jeremiah (who thought he was too young to be of use), from the gospel account of the Lord Jesus welcoming little children, and from his times at camp. This was how John Stott always argued his case. He would use biblical principles and then show from real life how they can be worked out.

The spiritual influences he had known in his own childhood had gone very deep. First, his mother who urged him to read his Bible and to pray; then Nanny Golden who taught him and Joy choruses and took them to Sunday School; and then Bash. One plants, another waters, and God gives the growth.

History in the making

Around the corner from Ridley Hall, in Selwyn Gardens, history was about to be made.

John's friend Oliver Barclay from Trinity, now Dr Oliver Barclay, had moved to live in London. He joined the staff of the Inter Varsity Fellowship, helping Christian Unions like the CICCU all around the country. Oliver returned to Cambridge for a weekend as he wanted to share some big news with John.

> **Oliver** DJ has been telling us about a new idea, and I think you'll be interested.

Douglas Johnson (always called DJ) was Oliver's boss. John knew DJ, and thought very highly of him. Oliver continued:

- **Oliver** He's been sharing his hopes and dreams. Last week he talked to the staff about the church scene around the country. He really knows his stuff.
- **John** Tell me more *[pouring them both a cup of tea]*. You're right. I *am* interested.

John and Oliver had often discussed Bible teaching in churches. They longed to see the Bible taught better on Sundays. John wanted to hear DJ's views. DJ was clear-sighted.

- **Oliver** Actually he didn't start with the churches. That was what made it so interesting. He started with the universities. Theological colleges like Ridley Hall.
- **John** *[handing Oliver his tea]* Sadly most theology lecturers around the country do not believe the Bible to be the word of God.
- **Oliver** Exactly! Which is why DJ wants to start there. If theology lecturers had been better taught when *they* were students, they would be better at training the students under them.
- **John** I could not agree more. Future lecturers have to be well-grounded in biblical truth. They need to be able to make a case for it.
- **Oliver** DJ used the *exact* same expression! We have to equip lecturers better in making a case for the authority of the Bible. And *if* we do that, we'll see real change trickle down to local churches.
- **John** So what's the big news you wanted to share?

Under DJ's leadership a few years earlier, the Inter-Varsity Fellowship had founded a publishing house, Inter-Varsity Press (IVP). It was still fairly small at this stage, but producing some first-rate titles. John was sure DJ would have more big ideas.

- **Oliver** To set up a theological research centre. He's already begun to discuss it with a few friends. They want it to be close to a university.

This was a *very* big idea! John offered Oliver a biscuit as he took in what Oliver was saying.

Oliver If you have half an hour, I'd like to show you a house which I think could fit the bill.

John Really?

['Really' was one of Oliver's favourite words. It could mean so many things, depending on its intonation. The two friends laughed.]

Oliver Yes. *Really!* It belongs to a distant cousin. I heard about it on the Barclay grapevine. Let me show you - it's in Selwyn Gardens.

John was keen to see it. When they finished their tea, they walked down Sidgwick Avenue and turned the corner into Grange Road. Cambridge would be a perfect location for such a venture. Standing outside the long, two-storey house in Selwyn Gardens, they wondered if God would bring DJ's dream to reality.

Oliver There's a lovely garden at the back *[leading the way around the side of the house]*.

John *[with a grin]* Room for expansion!

With the help of a generous donor, 36 Selwyn Gardens was purchased in 1944. Over the following years it became widely known as a centre for evangelical research, and drew some of the best evangelical minds in the world. The centre was called Tyndale House after William Tyndale, who translated much of the Bible into English. Tyndale House, under God, still plays a key role in the church.

John spent much time at Tyndale House during his final year in Cambridge, talking with its warden, and with the first students who were researching for doctorates. It was a small beginning. But men like DJ were visionaries; so they looked at what *was*, and saw what *could be*.

John naturally passed his exams. He could have been ordained in the summer of 1945, but a new Principal was arriving at Ridley Hall, and John thought it would be good to stay an extra term. He could assist the new Principal in settling in the new students, and he could get on with some more study, without the distraction of exams. So he wrote to his father, to see if his father would support him financially for this extra time.

His father's response was part of the wonderful mosaic God was painting. Arnold Stott did not consider theology to be part of John's real education. If John would spend the time reading more widely, then he liked the idea. So John planned to stay for the Michaelmas Term, to dip into new areas of study. John Stott became known for his wide intellectual reach, which was a hallmark of his preaching and his writing.

The extra term in Cambridge also brought a providential meeting, which would determine John's future. Harold Earnshaw-Smith, Rector of All Souls, where John had been taken to Sunday School by Nanny Golden, was the speaker at a special CICCU event toward the end of that term, and John was there.

Mr Earnshaw-Smith Have you lined up a curacy yet, John?

John No, not yet. I do need to give time to that.

Mr Earnshaw-Smith Would you like to come back to All Souls? Home territory for you, and lots of students around. I know you've been much valued in the CICCU.

London University had a Christian Union on the same model as Cambridge, with central meetings and college meetings. Many of its members came to All Souls. Mr Earnshaw-Smith was thinking aloud. And in his mind's eye he could see just the right role for John.

This invitation came out-of-the-blue for John. He said he would like to write to his father for advice. Arnold Stott wrote back to say he had no objection. Within a few weeks John, to his great surprise, was curate at All Souls, Langham Place.

John Stott left Cambridge at the age of 24. That summer was his last as Camp Secretary. His years in the CICCU and at camp had both left a deep mark on him, a mark he never forgot. Sixty years later he still described himself as 'a product of camps and the CICCU'. God had used them to form him.

John squeezed in a visit to camp each summer for many years, partly to catch up with friends, and partly to get to know new leaders. John was always looking ahead to see how people's skills could best be used.

Years after leaving Cambridge, both John and Oliver were asked to become lifetime Honorary Vice Presidents of CICCU. They accepted with pleasure.

Fascinating Fact 8

PLANNING AHEAD

When planning ahead with a goal in view, some ask the question 'How do we get there?' It's a good question, but it can be too vague.

A better question is: 'What do we need to do in the next year (or three years, or five years) to achieve our goal?' Having a firm goal in place, a plan of what needs to be done, and a commitment to do whatever it takes, is a great place for a Christian to be.

CHAPTER 6

A CURATE BECOMES HOMELESS (1945-1950)

In 1945, the Second World War came to an end. Victory was first announced in Europe, then a month later came VJ Day – victory over Japan. The victory of VJ Day had been won at a terrible cost, with atomic bombs on Hiroshima and Nagasaki. Some 200,000 people had died in the two cities.

Hard times lay ahead for everyone who survived the concentration camps, and for all those who had lost husbands, fathers and sons in the fighting. But now the country could once more plan ahead, and replenish its resources. The building industry was revived, and there were many new jobs in this area, and in other areas. Food rationing and clothes rationing were gradually phased out over the next few years. Life was beginning to get back to normal.

John had been in Cambridge for almost the entire war. Now he would be back on home territory, in the church where he had grown up. There was no house for a curate, and John's family had left Harley Street by this stage. Marcus Dukes, a friend from Rugby, came up with an idea.

    Marcus My parents will give you a room. I'm sure of it. There's a nice room at the top of the house, and you'd be comfortable there, with quiet to work.

    John Well I'd be very grateful if they could. It would be for just a few weeks. That will give me a chance to find something else.

Marcus I'll write to them today. You can't get much nearer than 1 Queen Anne Street!

Before leaving Cambridge, John sent out invitations to all his family and friends, inviting them to pray for him, and to come to the service where he would be ordained. The card read:

> Your prayers are asked for John R W Stott
> who is to be ordained deacon by the Bishop of London
> in St Paul's Cathedral at 9.30am
> on St Thomas's Day, Friday 21st December 1945,
> to serve in the parish of All Souls, Langham Place,
> and St Peter's, Vere Street, London W1.
>
> RIDLEY HALL, CAMBRIDGE   1 QUEEN ANNE STREET, LONDON W1

Robbie Bickersteth had died in the war in 1944. John's loss of this friend and mentor was huge. Robbie's widow, Penelope, wrote:

> How Robbie would have loved to be with you.

Hugh Lyon, the Headmaster at Rugby, also wrote. He recalled John's outstanding leadership of the Levée.

> You may be sure of my thoughts and prayers. I think you know what I wish for you and how happy I am about your decision.

This note may have gone a small way to helping John's father come to terms with John's calling. Both of John's parents came to the ordination, and so did Nanny Golden.

John's great-aunt Emily was thrilled to hear of John's conversion to Christ at Rugby, and now of his ordination. She wrote:

> You *daily* have my prayers

She enclosed some 'pearls of great price'. These were verses of scripture carefully-chosen and copied out. Many words were underlined in her elderly handwriting.

> **I send an angel before thee**
> **Shine as lights in the world**

> Ye know that your labour is not in vain
> I will never leave thee nor forsake thee

John was struck by her kindness, and would remember these verses.

Starting as a curate

All Souls Church, Langham Place, is just a few minutes' walk north from Oxford Circus, one of the busiest London Underground stations, and next to the BBC headquarters. Londoners working in offices nearby emerge from the Underground and walk past the church, day by day, week by week. Visitors to the capital teem around the local streets, shopping for souvenirs, visiting the BBC shop, or cutting through from Oxford Street to Regents Park and the Zoo. It is in a very busy spot.

John Stott moved into the top floor at 1 Queen Anne Street. The arrangement was meant to be short-term, but John got on so well with Dr and Mrs Cuthbert Dukes that it lasted for more than four years! It took John less than a minute to walk to All Souls and just a few minutes to walk to St Peter's, Vere Street, where he took many services.

While John had a privileged childhood, he was mindful of those who had much less privilege. At Rugby, before he became a Christian, he had founded the ABC society, to enable the homeless to have a bath. It was called by the simple initials ABC to help people with little education to remember it. When he became a Christian this sensitivity to the poor was sharpened even more. God is a God of justice and of mercy and of compassion for the poor and needy.

All Souls parish included extremes of wealth and poverty. The streets designed by John Nash housed families with much wealth. But other nearby streets, in the eastern area called Fitzrovia, were quite different. John would visit the elderly, and the sick, and the widows. He saw how some lived in very poor housing, often overcrowded.

Fitzrovia was becoming multiracial after the War. Spaniards, Italians and Cypriots had already moved into the area. Over the next ten years families from Asia and the Caribbean also arrived to seek a new life. The parish included a hostel for working boys, away from home for the first time. John enjoyed his visits to the hostel, and won the boys' confidence as he listened and talked, and tried to understand the way they thought.

The local children had neither the education nor the privileges he had enjoyed. He wanted to stretch their minds, and expand their experience. So he decided to take them camping. This was a major operation. He needed to borrow tents, sleeping bags, and cooking utensils. John's work as Camp Secretary was great preparation. He made lists of everything, planned simple menus, and took the boys on shopping expeditions for the food they were to eat.

The children loved going camping and John loved to take them. Each morning he would give them a wake-up call on his piano accordion. He no doubt tried to get them interested in bird-watching and in nature, to 'shut their mouths and open their eyes and ears', as he had learned to do.

John taught the children songs about Christ, so the words would sink down deeply. Even if he lost touch with them, and they lost touch with church, they would remember spiritual truth they learned in the songs. Each day he read the Bible with them. Altogether this was a wonderful break for these inner-city kids. They loved their curate. You could tell that by the way they laughed at his accent and mimicked him. John pronounced words with deliberate care and he 'landed' each sentence with a distinctive cadence. Intonation doesn't change much over the years, and John maintained this way of speaking all his life, as you can hear if you listen to him preaching online.

The children knew that Mr Stott, as they called him, had two middle names, beginning R and W. Surely they must be very grand names, the children thought. With gleeful humour, some children decided to guess them, and persuaded others that they were right. In this way a rumour spread that his full name was John Rochester Winchester Stott. Rochester and Winchester were the longest, grandest names the children could think of – they are the names of two cathedral cities in the south of England.

Every curate looks up to the vicar he serves under. How that vicar approaches his ministry will leave a lasting mark on the curate. This was the case with John, as he observed Harold Earnshaw-Smith. Mr Earnshaw-Smith loved Christ, and loved to speak of him, always wanting to test new ideas for evangelism. Then he would use the best ideas he could find to make the All Souls ministry as effective as it could be. He was a strong spiritual leader.

He also had a good sense of humour. Picture in your mind's eye a Sunday morning service in those days. New curates all took a turn at preaching, and prepared painstakingly. They needed to handle the Bible passage well, to teach it and apply it. In this way church members would be equipped as Christians in their job on a Monday morning. Such a large congregation in central London included specialists in just about every profession. There would be non-Christians present too, for whom the sermon was a stepping stone in understanding the Christian faith. The curates took sermon preparation very seriously.

Mr Earnshaw-Smith would enjoy playing a trick on his new curates, and it never failed.... During the singing of a hymn he would walk over and say 'You're preaching this morning, aren't you?' when he knew he was to preach himself! It took only a second to realize he was joking, but that heart-stopping second stayed in the curate's mind for a *very* long time!

John Stott's father was soon to be made a Knight, and therefore to become Sir Arnold Stott. John was very proud of his father's achievements, and the recognition he had been given. But this did not distract John from his work in the poorer part of the parish. John did not join his family for Christmas, as he knew some of the poor would have no-one to visit them. So on Christmas Eve and Christmas Day he would visit up to seventy or eighty homes, and leave in each a food parcel as a gift. This Christmas delivery of food parcels later grew into a system of regular visits to these homes by a team of church volunteers. The poor in the parish always remained a priority for John.

One day a vagrant called Harry Mossop approached John Stott after a service. Could he have some money? John had a rule of not giving money to tramps; instead he would offer them food, and talk with them. So he invited Harry Mossop round to his home. Harry visited John in his home often, over several years, and they would eat together, and John would open the Bible and pray.

An experiment

Around this time John Stott decided to do an experiment. It was October or November, when the nights began early. He didn't shave for a few days, then he put on some very old clothes, and walked into the cold, dark evening. No one knew where he had gone. He made his way down Upper Regent Street, past Oxford Circus, and on down Regent Street. With hands in pockets to keep them as warm as possible, he crossed Trafalgar Square. He was about to see what London looked like through the eyes of the homeless. It was important that no-one find out. He didn't want anyone bringing him hot soup, or sandwiches. He wanted to experience, insofar as he could, *exactly* what it was like to be homeless, and to have no-one really care.

Under Charing Cross Bridge, several homeless men and women had begun to bed down for the night. There were no blankets – just newspapers to keep them warm over their clothes. The pavement beneath was hard and cold. John had no newspapers with him as he hadn't thought of looking for any on the way. So he just found a gap, lay down, and tried to make himself comfortable, which wasn't easy. He didn't sleep much – people were coming and going, because they couldn't sleep either. Some were making a lot of noise because they were drunk.

The next day he walked through the East End and was glad to find a patch of ground where he could lie on the grass and doze. He spent the following night in the Whitechapel Salvation Army hostel. Putting on his best cockney accent, he managed to get a bed. But it was another sleepless night, with a lot of drunken noise. In the morning he decided he had seen all he needed to see. He now knew what it felt like to be cold and hungry, and not able to sleep. He was very glad to return home. His friend Marcus's parents in Queen Anne Street, like John, had a strong social conscience, and they listened eagerly as he told his story.

By this time Mr Earnshaw-Smith had become ill, and John Stott was carrying a lot of responsibility for the church. His diary was jammed. He would often be seen to jump on his bike and cycle off to speak at student Christian Union meetings, giving himself just the time he needed to get there. Oliver Barclay was delighted to see John still speaking to student groups. Oliver was now married, and he and his family worshipped at All Souls.

In March 1950, when John Stott was still 28, a great shock swept through the whole church family. Harold Earnshaw-Smith, their much-loved Rector, died in his sleep. He had been ill for a while, and it was hoped he would recover. John had written to him shortly before he died; he was concerned for him and wanted to relieve Mr Earnshaw-Smith of some of his load. But in God's providence, Mr Earnshaw-Smith went to be with Christ, and history was to take an unexpected turn. All Souls Church was now seeking a new Rector.

The churchwardens drew up the profile of the person they believed All Souls needed. These days, with large team ministries, the Rector does not need to be able to do everything well, but the All Souls team then was very small. This, in essence, was the profile:

> **PROFILE OF NEW RECTOR FOR ALL SOULS CHURCH**
>
> - He should be a fine preacher.
> - He should be able to handle the business of the church well, and be an excellent administrator.
> - He should love to work among the poor, as there are many poor families in the parish.
> - He should work well among young people with a special interest in the children's clubs.

Rectors of All Souls Church are not appointed by the Bishop of London, as might be expected, but by the Crown. First, the Prime Minister (then Clement Attlee) had to recommend a name to King George VI. As a first step, George Cansdale (a member of the church council, and Superintendent of London Zoo) went with the churchwardens to 10 Downing Street. Here they presented the profile to Anthony Bevir, who assisted the Prime Minister with church appointments.

The churchwardens were clear in their minds. They wanted to see John Stott appointed. Curates would not normally become rector of the church they served, so it was seen as an unusual suggestion. Not only that, but John was only 29 years old and All Souls was a landmark church in London's West End. Would the Prime Minister trust their judgment?

Anthony Bevir listened intently, as they made their case. It would be a high-risk strategy, in human terms, to place such a young man in this role. References were read, forms filled out, telephone calls made, internal memos written. Then Anthony Bevir met with the Prime Minister. Let's imagine their conversation.

Anthony Bevir Prime Minister, John Stott is an unusual candidate. He is the present curate, young and inexperienced.

Prime Minister How old is he?

Anthony Bevir He's 29, Prime Minister. But the churchwardens are neither young nor inexperienced, and they think he will do a fine job. George Cansdale came with them to meet with me.

Prime Minister The Zoo man?

Anthony Bevir Yes, Prime Minister. These men work closely with him, and I think we need to take their recommendation seriously.

Prime Minister Well, if Cansdale can run a zoo, he must know something about running a church.

Anthony Bevir was a diligent man who researched everything carefully before bringing it to the Prime Minister. Clement Attlee knew this, so despite the fact that John was only 29 years old, he agreed.

Prime Minister Make sure Stott is willing to have his name go forward, then kindly draft a letter from me to the King.

Anthony Bevir Yes, Prime Minister.

Things moved quickly, and within four days the King accepted the nomination. The July 1950 issue of the All Souls church newsletter opened with a simple announcement:

OUR NEW RECTOR

His Majesty the King has been graciously pleased to appoint the Reverend J R W STOTT MA to the living of All Souls, Langham Place.

The news of this appointment has been received with joy and thankfulness by the whole church.

The Churchwardens

Fascinating Fact 9

REFLECTIONS ON CHRISTIAN MINISTRY

Ordination is a serious matter, a commitment to God for a life of ministry. Over forty years later, on John Stott's 70th birthday, he reflected on the theme of 'verses to live by', and preached that week at All Souls from Malachi 2. The second verse of this chapter was another verse he had sought to live by. This is what he said, with the words slightly updated:

The best motto I can think of for anyone in Christian service is in this verse. 'Lay it to heart to give glory to God's name.' It became in a sense my motto. In Christian leadership or ministry, we should not be concerned about the glory of our own silly little name, but about the glory of the name of God.'

The verses sent to John by his great aunt Emily stayed with him all his life.

Chapter 7
All Souls Rector
(1950-1970)

PART 1

John Stott's time as Rector of All Souls Church covered some of the most interesting years in Britain. In 1950, five years after the end of the Second World War, most families were still living without much money. They would look for clothes or furniture in second-hand shops more often than buying them new. Few people had cars, and televisions were only just starting to appear in homes. As the 1960s began to unfold, so did a new Britain. There are many books written about the 1960s, when names like The Beatles, The Rolling Stones, Jimi Hendrix and Woodstock changed the music scene. If you want to understand the world your grandparents grew up in, it is worth knowing about this zany and fast-moving decade.

But let's not rush ahead. In the summer of 1950 John Stott packed up his things in 1 Queen Anne Street, to move into the Rectory, at 12 Weymouth Street, five minutes' walk away. But what would he do with all the space? Since leaving home he had been used to student rooms in Cambridge, and then a bedsitter. Now he was moving into a house with a basement and five floors above it! After careful thought, he came up with an idea. He would invite curates, or single men in the congregation, to live in the house. All he needed to keep for himself was a bedroom and a study. He met with his churchwardens to ask what they thought.

'We would still use the drawing room for church meetings during the week,' he explained. This was the room from which he had so often been excluded (with his toy daggers and guns) while in Sunday School.

The churchwardens and the church council agreed. It was an unusual plan for a Rectory, but it made good sense. John began looking for housemates, and for a housekeeper and a cook.

Everyone had breakfast in the communal dining room in the basement, and everyone met there again for their evening meal. Those who lived there called it 'The Wreckage' (a cross between a rectory and a vicarage) or sometimes rather cheekily 'The Stottery'. John Stott reported how well it was working in the All Souls newsletter. He enjoyed playing with words, and, joining now the *beginning* of Vicarage with the *end* of Rectory, he stated: 'The Wreckage is a Victory'. And so it was.

John Stott could not forget his two days as a tramp. It was no fun to be homeless. Harry Mossop still visited regularly for a meal. If John found himself in conversation after church with a man needing help, he invited the man home, gave up his own bed, and slept on a camp bed in his study.

With Harley Street specialists in one direction, and poor families in another, All Souls would always have to serve both, as well as shopworkers, businessmen, students… John was called by God to be pastor to those from each group, rich and poor, educated and uneducated. He wanted to make sure everyone was cared for.

In those days, the church congregation sat in pews. These were wooden benches with a back, all beautifully varnished, and with a little door at the end, to box it in. All Souls, like many other churches, set aside pews for families to rent each year for £60, if they so wished. (That was a huge amount of money then.) Families who could afford the money liked to know they could sit in the same place every week. But this troubled John. What if new people came into church and sat in a reserved pew without realizing, and then had to be asked to move? This would make people feel very awkward. Free seating everywhere was the only answer. He persuaded the church council that this was the way to go, and they agreed.

Not everyone in church was happy, but John knew it was right.

One day a new family appeared in church. They were evidently not poor. The oldest daughter had become a Christian while living in France. Now she was home with her parents again, and she wanted to join a church. She had a younger brother and sister, and they started to come with her each Sunday. John would always be at the back of the church to greet people as they left, and he got to know them. One Sunday he decided to invite the two younger children to tea in Weymouth Street. After tea, the plan was for him to talk with the girl and for his curate, John Collins, his friend from Cambridge days, to talk with the boy. Bash always sought a one-to-one conversation, and that was how John himself had come to faith at Rugby, so he tried to do this whenever he could. The children evidently appreciated it, and came back to the next Guest Service in church with their whole family. The girl, who was 14 at the time, wrote afterwards:

> Wasn't it wizard that the parents came to your last 'Guest Service'. It was a terrific fight, but they came eventually!! Mr Eddison [the other curate] said on the previous Sunday that everyone should bring a person with them, so I got Mummy, my brother got Granny, and Daddy just came! They enjoyed it very much; and Mummy now says that church-going becomes a habit!!
>
> When are you coming over, because the parents want to talk with you, and if you come for an afternoon and evening you can do some birdwatching.
>
> Lots of love

Life was very, very busy. John preached regularly, spoke at many events around the country, and handled a huge amount of correspondence. If people came to see him, he would allot each one half-an-hour and give them his full attention. After twenty-five minutes, it was time to close the conversation with prayer, and to turn his mind to the next person, who also needed undivided attention. And so the days were filled.

John picked up an idea around this time which changed the way he worked. The idea was really very simple. From then on he set aside one day a month for a Quiet Day away from the Wreckage. He left early, and did not get back until bedtime. This day gave him space for unhurried thought. Perhaps a letter needed a careful response, or an article had to be written – or he had a new idea to evaluate. This Quiet Day would go into his diary with a capital Q.

That was all. But he knew what it stood for, and he would guard the day from any other intrusion. At one stage the monthly Q became a weekly Q. It was his lifeline. He said (though not publicly) that he would rather have this weekly Quiet Day than a day off, if he ever had to make a choice.

John's mind was a breeding ground for new ideas. He needed time to bring them to the Lord and choose priorities. One idea which needed thought and prayer was very adventurous. Maybe, just maybe, All Souls should purchase a property close to the All Souls Primary School, to be used for the children's work. (All Souls Primary School, linked to the church, served the poorer part of the parish.) Such a venture would cost a *lot* of money, as it would need to be furnished and equipped, and they would also need someone to run it. If they did have a building near the school, perhaps Sunday services could be held in it too. 'Imagine,' John thought to himself as he leaned back in his chair and looked out of the window. 'A church without pews!' This was very daring for its day.

In November 1958 the house at 139 Cleveland Street was opened as the All Souls Clubhouse. Tom Robinson from Canada was its first warden. As many as 392 children and young people came to the Opening. Many knew John Stott, and he knew most of them, though hardly any had ever come to All Souls. In due course Tom built a team of volunteers to help him run activities. On Christmas Day the Clubhouse served Christmas dinner to anyone who would be on their own for Christmas. The Clubhouse was very close to John Stott's heart and he would go there for Christmas dinner whenever he could manage to.

John Stott was like a mental and a social 'gymnast'. He was agile in hopping between the uneducated and the highly-educated, and between dropouts and those in the highest ranks of society. Society was much more formal in those days, and church members and people outside the church all called him Rector, or Mr Stott. But slowly he began to be known as Uncle John, first by students and then more widely. It was a name which showed respect, while also showing affection, and a name which would travel around the world. As the years went by, he was often referred to simply as 'UJ'.

PART 2

Uncle John studied the Bible diligently, as God's Word for his world. He also studied God's world. He became well known for this. He read widely, so he could grasp what the leaders and influencers (or movers and shakers) of the day were saying. The extra term which he had spent in Cambridge had laid a wonderful foundation for this.

'We need to give time to understanding ideas,' he said to his church staff one week at their meeting. 'Ideas shape the way we think, and the way we think shapes the way we behave.'

Uncle John wanted to find out *why* people didn't believe in Jesus, and what obstacles they had to believing. He wanted both his writing and his preaching to engage with real life - in schools, in the street, in the office, and in the university common rooms.

'Intellectual pride is a terrible thing,' Uncle John went on. 'People succeed at university, and become doctors, bankers, and professors. They think they do not need God. What the Apostle Paul preached and wrote on this is a great inspiration to me.'

The staff could see why straight away. The Apostle was a master in talking to the intellectuals of his day. (We can read his famous address to the great university city of Athens in Acts 17.) Skilfully he takes his listeners from what they know, and introduces them to what they *don't* know. The Apostle Paul followed Christ with a passion. Three times in the New Testament he uses the phrase '*my* gospel', as it was so precious to him. He had committed his whole life to the gospel. The Apostle Paul was Uncle John's model as a thinker, and as a leader.

In the period following the Second World War, Britain was much more Christian than it is now. Some London businessmen decided to invite an American evangelist to come to Britain, and, in faith, they booked the huge Harringay Stadium. This evangelist was called Billy Graham.

Billy Graham's first visit to Britain

Each night thousands poured into the stadium. Churches within a 50-mile radius hired coaches. All Souls Church took busloads, night after night. Many people invited friends and family, just like the girl who thought it was 'wizard' that her parents came to the Guest Service. There were adverts on the London Underground and on the city buses; there were newspaper adverts, and there were adverts on billboards around the suburbs. This visit of Billy Graham was *massive* news, and often on the front page of newspapers. Uncle John was at Harringay every night, leading the way, and inviting people to go.

Frances Whitehead

The more Uncle John did, the more there was to do. Letters arrived at an alarming rate. He was being asked to speak at meetings around the UK and around the world. Uncle John needed a secretary to answer these letters, type articles and books, and field telephone calls. This would be a frontline role, relating to church leaders, to missionaries, and to organizers of events and conferences. His new secretary would have to be highly efficient. She would also need to understand what John was doing, and have a good grasp of the evangelical faith.

A young woman called Frances Whitehead had been coming to All Souls for a few years. She worked at the BBC. Frances had gone through the ten-week course for new Christians, and was now teaching a group herself. After thinking and praying about her future, she was wondering whether she should leave the BBC and go to Bible College, so she made an appointment to speak with John Stott about it after work one Friday. John listened, then came up with a different idea – perhaps Frances should become his secretary. Frances thought he was joking. She was disappointed that he didn't think Bible College was a good idea, as she had hoped to receive his encouragement for the plan, but she tried to put it out of her mind as she cycled home.

Less than a week later, the phone rang in her office, where she worked for a BBC Producer. She picked up the receiver, and was taken completely by surprise, as she recognized the voice straight away.

John Stott Hello Frances.

Frances Oh, hello Mr Stott.

John Stott Well, have you thought about it?

Frances Thought about what?

John Stott About coming to be my secretary.

Frances No! I didn't think you were serious!

Frances agreed to think and pray about this new role. She had come to faith in Christ only three years earlier, and she didn't have background knowledge of anything the Rector did. But a week later, sensing it was the right thing to do, Frances gave in her notice at the BBC. The year was 1956.

Frances picked things up fast and soon became central to everything John Stott did. Uncle John started to call her 'the omnicompetent Frances'. Neither of them could have imagined that they would work together for the rest of Uncle John's long life. In 1983 the Archbishop of Canterbury awarded Uncle John a doctorate, the Lambeth Doctor of Divinity; and in 2001 the Archbishop awarded Frances a Lambeth MA. This shows the huge contribution Frances Whitehead made to John Stott's ministry.

PART 3

When Uncle John travelled to other countries, he often said to new friends he made, 'Come and stay at the Wreckage if you're in London.' This was typical of his generous nature.

When speaking at a university mission in Kenya, he got to know a student called David Gitari (whom we meet properly in Chapter Nine). David was chairman of the committee which had invited John to speak. Later David came to study in the UK, and he stayed in Weymouth Street for a month when he first arrived. During that time he saw Uncle John only once, when they arranged to have breakfast together. 'It was amazing to me, as an African,' he said, 'that I could stay in a friend's house for a whole month, and see him only once, and that by appointment!'

Uncle John would be up early in the morning. With his busy diary, and the need to wedge in time to think as well as time to write, he couldn't always join others when they gathered for meals. The only way he could manage to do everything was to guard his time carefully – or, more accurately, for Frances to guard his time. She did so like a lioness. No-one could get past Frances when Uncle John was focusing on writing or preparation. And that meant no-one. It was not unusual for a conversation like this to take place.

(phone ringing)

Frances Hello, John Stott's Secretary here.

Voice Hi, I'm in London this week, from the USA. Please could I arrange a few minutes with John Stott?

Frances I'm sorry but that won't be possible.

Voice Is he out of town? I thought he was here at the moment.

Frances Yes, he is here, but his time is already given to preparation for upcoming meetings.

Voice Oh, I just meant five or ten minutes. It doesn't need to be long.

Frances No, I'm sorry, that won't be possible. He is seeing only those who have made appointments, and his diary is full.

Voice Well, could I just talk with him briefly on the phone?

Frances No, as I've said, he's very busy.

And so it would go on. No-one could ever get past Frances. Two of the Wreckage residents thought they would have some fun by seeing if they could manage – it was already a sport among the curates, who would try to imitate the accents of some of Uncle John's senior friends from overseas, but none had succeeded. Could John Smith and David Wells pull it off?

John Smith takes up the story:

> I borrowed some props from other residents – a dog collar and black stock, an old raincoat and a trilby, then I blacked out one of my front teeth with a Chinograph pencil, removed my spectacles and rang the doorbell. As planned, David Wells passed Frances's office to answer the door before she could get there, and let me into the entrance hall. When Frances heard conversation below, she rushed down the stairs to investigate, only to be greeted by this unknown reverend gentleman who had come to see Mr Stott.
>
> As I held out my hand and greeted Frances with my fictitious name, she did not recognize me and appeared very perturbed. She insisted that there was no possibility of my seeing Mr Stott that day, nor any other, without an appointment. I feigned perplexity, but could not retain my poise and within a few seconds surrendered. Her Majesty was not amused! Typical of Frances, she was immediately forgiving – and when I checked some years later, the prank was erased from her memory.

Radical changes

In 1970, after 20 years with a heavily-packed schedule, John Stott realized the need for radical change. He talked with Frances Whitehead about this. Frances was feeling under huge pressure, too. She was the All Souls church secretary, and at the same time supporting John in his growing travels around the country and overseas. Uncle John felt that he wasn't giving enough time to his curates, or to the church; and the invitations kept coming. What should he do?

An old friend, Dick Lucas, whom he had known for many years, was Rector of St Helen's Church in Bishopsgate, in the City of London. St Helen's was growing significantly, and Dick understood the needs of a central London church. He and Uncle John would meet for breakfast when they could. Over their next breakfast together, John shared this problem.

> **UJ** I am under terrific pressure, with so many invitations to speak, and committees to chair. Frances is feeling it too. She is the church secretary, she types my books, and she arranges my travels, which always include a complicated itinerary to make the most of being in that country.
>
> **Dick** Yes, I can see how pressured this must be. Being innovators, as we both are, means more pressure on us, and on the people who work with us.
>
> **UJ** I'm wondering if I should invite someone else to lead All Souls, so Frances and I can give our energies solely to the international work.
>
> **Dick** That would be a radical plan, and you would need to delegate the running of the church to him completely. But to me it makes good sense.

Uncle John valued Dick's advice.

> **UJ** Do you have ideas whom I could ask?
>
> **Dick** What about Michael Baughen?
>
> **UJ** Yes, of course! I hadn't thought of him. Thank you, Dick. Michael certainly has the gifts needed. I wonder if he would come.

Both knew that Michael Baughen had just completed a big building project at Holy Trinity, Platt in Manchester. Would he want to move? And what about his family? It would be a very big change for them to come to central London.

> **UJ** I'll talk with him, and ask him to think and pray about it.

So Uncle John wrote to his friend, and asked if they could meet next time Michael was in London. Michael Baughen and his wife, Myrtle, were in for a surprise.

Frances drove Michael to the station after his meeting with Uncle John. She more than anyone knew the pressures John was under, and urged Michael to accept, which he did. It was a wrench to leave Manchester, but Michael and Myrtle sensed it was God's leading. So Uncle John and the churchwardens invited Michael Baughen to become vicar of All Souls, and to lead the church's ministry. But they couldn't invite him to become the Rector, taking all the responsibility, as only Queen Elizabeth could do that. The Baughen family moved into the Rectory in 1970. Five years later Michael was appointed fully as Rector, at the invitation of the Queen. John Stott, by then 49 years old, became Rector Emeritus.

This meant that in 1970 everyone had to move out of the Wreckage, to turn it back into a Rectory. A small mews flat was built for Uncle John over the garage at the back of the house, facing down Bridford Mews. Immediately above the garage was John's bedroom and shower room (no room for a bath), and on the second floor a simple living room and small kitchen. The living room had bookshelves right along one wall, and John placed his desk in front of a large bay window overlooking the mews. The front door was at 13 Bridford Mews, but hardly anyone used that. Most people came up the stairs from the Rectory. This meant walking through Uncle John's bedroom. So his bedroom doubled as a corridor for visitors who used the Rectory entrance.

Frances's desk had been in the sunny Drawing Room. She now moved into what had been the cook's bedroom on the ground floor. When people came to see Uncle John, she would show them up to his sitting room, through his bedroom. It was a modest home, but John didn't keep anything he didn't use. So this space was all he needed.

Fascinating Fact 10

THREE DIRECTIONS NOT CHOSEN

There were three directions in life which John Stott did not pursue. Had he followed any one of them, his life would have been different. Each would have been good in itself, but Uncle John sensed that none was in God's plan for him.

First, he did not become a Bishop, though he was pressed to do so from when he was a young rector.

Secondly, he did not teach in a university, though he could have become a Professor in one of the world's best-known.

Thirdly, he did not marry. There were two times in his life when he wondered if he might marry, but on each occasion he drew back, sensing it was not God's will for him.

His millions of miles travelled, and his millions of words written required freedom from these responsibilities.

Fascinating Fact 11

FRANCES WHITEHEAD

Frances Whitehead (1925-2019) did secret maths work in the Second World War. She had a very good mind.

Frances typed all of John Stott's books from longhand. While she carried the title 'secretary' it did not reflect her level of responsibility. At the Thanksgiving service for her life, held in All Souls Church, Chris Wright described her partnership with Uncle John as 'one of the greatest partnerships in church history'.

Her biography *John Stott's Right Hand: The untold story of Frances Whitehead* (Dictum, updated 2020) is a story Uncle John hoped would one day be told. It is widely agreed that Uncle John could not have been half so effective without Frances at his right hand. She was known around the world as Auntie Frances. A library in El Salvador is named after her.

Fascinating Fact 12

INVENTOR OF THE MORSE CODE

Samuel Morse, the American inventor of the Morse code, was born in New England, in the state of Massachusetts. He sailed over to London to study in 1812, at the age of 21, and for three years he lived in Fitzrovia. Morse lodged at 141 Cleveland Street, next-door to the house All Souls Church purchased over a hundred years later for its 'church with no pews' experiment. He and John Stott shared the same birthday, 27 April.

Fascinating Fact 13

READING THE WHOLE BIBLE

In Uncle John's early days as Rector, Dr Martyn Lloyd-Jones the minister of Westminster Chapel (close to Buckingham Palace) handed him a small booklet. It was a reading plan covering the whole Bible, created by Robert Murray McCheyne, a Scottish minister who died in 1843, aged 29. He compiled this reading plan for his own church members in St Peter's, Dundee. It begins with the four 'great beginnings' in Scripture – Genesis (the birth of the universe), Ezra (the rebirth of the nation after Babylonian captivity), Matthew (the birth of Christ) and Acts (the birth of the body of Christ). It is now probably the widest-used reading plan in the world.

John was touched by the gift from Martyn Lloyd-Jones, whom he admired and respected. He began to use it straight away. He loved it, and he used it day-by-day, year-by-year, for the rest of his life, often giving copies away to friends. The reading plan was published again by Dictum Press when Uncle John was elderly. Uncle John wrote a piece at the front. It finishes: 'Nothing has helped me more than this to grasp the grand themes of the Bible.'

Fascinating Fact 14

CHAPLAIN TO THE QUEEN

In 1959 Frances opened an unexpected letter, with a royal crest on the envelope. She read it, and smiled. It was an invitation to John Stott to be a Chaplain to Her Majesty the Queen. The Queen has 36 chaplains at any one time, and the role is an honorary one. (It *didn't* mean that Uncle John would be pastor to the royal family.)

Chaplains to the Queen each preached annually at the chapel royal in St James's Palace, but the Queen was very rarely there. Some Chaplains never met the royal family. However the Queen *did* invite John Stott to meet with her. He spent a weekend as the Queen's guest at Sandringham, went to lunch with her at Buckingham Palace, and preached in front of the royal family more than once. The Queen evidently appreciated his ministry.

Chaplains to the Queen wear a rich scarlet cassock. George Cansdale wrote to the All Souls congregation, inviting members, if they wished, to contribute half-a-crown (equivalent of about £5 now) towards the purchase of these robes. The church family gladly gave. When John Stott's turn came to retire from his position, the Queen invited him to remain, and take the role of Extra Chaplain for the rest of his life. This invitation is a particular honour, extended to very few.

Chapter 8

Escaping to the Hookses (1952 onwards)

Rewind back to 1952.

John was standing in Bridford Mews, with his head inside his 'jalopy'. He loved to get away to remote areas on holiday. The more remote the better. This dated back to his birding trips with Robbie Bickersteth when he was a boy. Today he was leaving for holiday, and John Collins, his curate, was going with him. They were heading west, as far as they could get.

Uncle John   We're almost ready. Just checking we've got everything. Something to cook with, something to cook on, tent pegs, sleeping bag…

John Collins   Books to read, walking shoes, binoculars. Can't think of much else that matters.

Soon they were on their way, and leaving the urban sprawl.

Uncle John   It's good to have four wheels. Before I got the jalopy, I went up to Scotland once with a friend who had a motor bike.

John Collins   Sounds a long way on the back of a bike.

Uncle John We got the train to Carlisle. That's when the real adventure started. We took a bend too fast and we were both thrown off. I lost consciousness. He thought he'd killed me!

Eventually they reached Pembrokeshire, in West Wales. John drew into a lay-by and they looked at the map. 'Let's head for Dale,' he said. Dale is a village some ten or twelve miles from Haverfordwest. This was a journey he would make hundreds of times in the future, but he did not know that then.

It was a gloomy afternoon and beginning to rain. When the men reached Dale, they decided to look for somewhere to stay for their first night. The postmistress directed them up a hill to a farm.

'You can doss down in that nissen hut, if you like,' said the farmer. Just mind my sacks of potatoes.' It was shelter, and that was good enough.

Walking along the coastal path the next day, John and John saw many species of birds. Skomer and Skokholm islands lay about five miles offshore, world-famous breeding grounds. John took his binoculars everywhere. Now he and John Collins would be stopping every few minutes to catch a good view of the bird life.

While on holiday, Uncle John wanted to create a framework for a series of talks he would deliver three months later in Cambridge University. The talks had been arranged by the CICCU. John Collins was the ideal person to use as a sounding board as he, too, knew Cambridge well.

'Give me a couple of hours to make a start on the framework,' John Stott said. 'I'll sit over there.'

Praying for God's help, he sat down in warm sunshine, below the cliff top, leaning against the wall of a derelict farmhouse. His view was stunning.

John Collins went for a walk on his own, later joining John Stott where he was sitting.

Uncle John *[musing half to himself and half to John Collins]* I wonder who owns this farmhouse.

John Collins It is a tantalizing place, isn't it? Fabulous view across the bay.

Over the next few days they found out more about it. It was called The Hookses, though no-one knew where the name came from.

Uncle John If it ever comes up for sale, I think I'd try to buy it. I'm not sure how, but I'd love to try.

It was in a poor state, but its walls—nearly 30 inches thick—would withstand anything. John left his address with the local agent, just in case it ever came on the market.

A year or so passed, then a letter arrived. The Hookses was for sale! The owner had already turned down an offer of £1000, and Uncle John was advised to offer £1200. The estate agent thought it could be suitable for a café in the National Park. Uncle John shuddered at the prospect. Over the following week he made phone calls from London, and arranged a survey of the property. The result wasn't good. So he put in an offer of £500, hoping no one else would be interested. Alas, he lost The Hookses. Peter Conder, Warden of Skokholm, offered £800 and became its new owner. Uncle John was disappointed. However, that is not the end of the story.

A few months later, Peter Conder was appointed Director of the Royal Society for the Protection of Birds (RSPB) and had to move to be nearer London. Uncle John had just completed his first book *Men with a Message*, and received £750 from its publisher. So with it, he purchased The Hookses from Peter Conder. A few months later, he felt it wasn't fair to have bought it at less than Mr Conder paid for it, so he invited him to lunch, and handed him £50.

A gale that winter took off the roof (happily Peter Conder's insurance was still in place). There was no mains electricity, no mains water, and no fence to mark the boundary to the property. In short, it was in a sad state. Ah, but that was not the way Uncle John perceived it! For, like his older friend DJ, he was a visionary. He looked at what *was*, and saw what *could be*. Here in his mind's eye he could see his writing retreat; a place for study, and for relaxation; a place to invite friends; a place for students to come...

'What about coming to The Hookses for a working holiday?' John asked his family and friends. 'Bring your old clothes and wellies.' There was a lot of hard work to do, both inside and outside. Together they mixed concrete, dug the garden, pulled out weeds and sludge from the pond, and painted walls and doors. Over the years, The Hookses was completely transformed.

How The Hookses was transformed

Uncle John wrote most of his books at The Hookses. He would set apart several weeks per year, and travel down alone or with friends. Frances would transfer her office to Dale too. They and their friends came to be regarded as part of the local community, and they got to know the Christians who worshipped at the village church.

The Hookses now is what Uncle John saw in his mind's eye back in 1952, through generous gifts from friends, and a lot of hard work. Overlooking the bay is UJ's desk, on roughly the same spot where he sat down in 1952 to think and pray about his talks for the Cambridge University mission. The outbuilding he had been leaning against was transformed into 'The Hermitage', a flat with a bedroom, a study, and a sitting room / cum office for Frances. With the help of some friends, John laid the concrete path leading to The Hermitage. He named it with a grin 'The Frances Whitehead Walkway'.

The Hookses—the main house and outbuildings—can accommodate 15 people. Its rooms are named after friends and family: for example Joanna's Room (after John's older sister Joanna), Joy's Room (after his sister Joy), Evelyn's Room, Meg's Loft, and Fanny's Room. (Fanny was Joy's beloved beagle 'as bad in character as it was good in looks'.)

John would work at his desk in The Hermitage, facing out towards the bay. When he had guests, he reached to the shelf on his right before he left his study. There, at arm's level, was one of his favourite books. He bought it while he was still at school. It was his copy of Saki's short stories. He loved these stories, and he loved to share them with others. He would laugh at them again and again, even though he had read them many times. Sometimes he would laugh so much at what was *about* to happen that he couldn't read any further! And the friends listening would laugh at him laughing! Soon everyone was laughing, but only John knew what was funny!

'Time for a Saki story,' he would say after dinner. If his friends were at The Hookses for the first time, and hadn't heard it before, he would begin with his favourite *The Lumber Room*. It is about a boy who said there was a frog in his bread-and-milk. His aunt punished him for making up the story. He had put the frog there himself, so he spoke with authority on the matter. His revenge on his aunt was very sweet. Saki's stories are still available from libraries. (Saki's real name was H H Munro but his books always carry the name Saki.)

'Double listening'

Uncle John loved Saki for relaxation, but his reading was not always so light-hearted.

Each day began with Bible reading, following the famous McCheyne reading plan. John wanted to master the whole Bible. Or rather, he wanted the whole Bible to master him. It is through reading scripture and studying it that Christians get to know God. Through Bible study, John Stott gained God's perspective on the world.

Uncle John wanted to persuade people that Christ is the Truth, and that the Christian faith affects all of life. To help him understand how people thought, so he could engage better with their questions, he read articles in newspapers, and watched plays and films. (This was in the days before the internet.) John knew the need to listen carefully to what people believed, as well as listening to what God says in the Bible. It was important to listen in both directions, each for a different reason. So he coined a new phrase – 'double listening'.

How a book led to a police chase

John Stott wrote over 50 books, all in longhand. The book John always considered his best was *The Cross of Christ*. He was 65 years old when it was published, and he dedicated it to Frances Whitehead. This book was translated into more than twenty languages. One of its many readers was Ajith Fernando. Ajith lives in Sri Lanka and, like Uncle John, loves to work among young people. Ajith travels widely, and speaks often, so he has to fit in reading where he can. Like Uncle John, he would be seen balancing books on his lap in airports, or he would read books or journals while standing at a bus stop.

Ajith Fernando loved *The Cross of Christ*. He spent four months reading it slowly and making notes in the margins. He underlined words and sentences, and even made an index at the back so he could find things again easily. He learned so much from the book. One day Ajith was travelling by bus through the mountains in Sri Lanka. The journey wasn't easy as the roads were bumpy, and full of bends. The bus was full, so Ajith had to stand. He couldn't read while the bus was travelling, because he had to hold on tightly with both hands. But each time the bus stopped for a few minutes, for passengers to get on or off, Ajith reached for the book, which he placed on a ledge. Then all of a sudden, while the bus was moving, he realized his precious book had fallen out of the bus. Disaster! So he quickly grabbed his bag, asked the driver to stop, and got out to hunt for it.

It was too late. The book had gone. Someone on a bus coming the other way had spotted it, and picked it up.

But just then a police jeep appeared. Ajith waved to the police to stop.

'I have just lost a book,' Ajith said in Singhalese, his local language. 'It fell out of the bus, and someone has picked it up, and it's now on a bus going that way!' The police were very understanding.

'Quick! Jump in!' the driver said.

'That's the bus!' said Ajith as they spotted it. The bus had stopped in the next town and Ajith was able to get his precious book back. He thanked the police warmly. The notes Ajith had written could not have been replaced. This shows the value placed on John Stott's books around the world.

Fascinating Fact 15

JOHN STOTT'S BOOKS

John Stott's books have reached many countries and have been read by millions of people. In total, they are translated into more than sixty languages. As new books came out – and sometimes even *before* they came out – publishers around the world would buy the rights to publish them. Uncle John's second book *Basic Christianity* grew out of his addresses at the Cambridge University Mission. This book alone sold over two-and-a-half million copies.

Book authors earn a 'royalty'. A royalty is a small payment for each book which is sold. All John Stott's royalties were (to use his own expression) 'recycled'. The money he gained from writing books was given to what is now known as Langham Literature. Through Langham Literature, books could be purchased for people in poorer countries, especially for pastors. Uncle John could have lived very comfortably on his royalties alone, but he chose not to keep any royalties. He accepted only a modest living allowance.

Fascinating Fact 16

CHANGING THE WAY PEOPLE THINK

If people think this life is all there is, their priority is to have fun and make money to enjoy themselves. So teenagers work hard to save up for an iphone, or computer software, or clothes, or a flatscreen TV for their room, or a motor bike or a car. Their parents work hard to upgrade their computer, buy a bigger house, or have more family holidays. These families won't be able to come to church on Sundays as they will be working, or shopping, or playing sport. They won't want to change this way of living, unless they can be persuaded that their way of *thinking* is wrong.

John Stott wanted to know *why* people believed what they did, for what we *believe* governs how we *behave*. And the way Christians behave plays a big part in how open we are to the Christian faith.

Chapter 9

Students, Students and more Students!

John Stott had laughed out loud in his student days, when Oliver Barclay had told him about his plans for post-graduate research.

> **John** *(In disbelief)* You're going to spend three years studying knee joints in *frogs*?'
>
> **Oliver** *(Trying to sound more persuasive)* Not just frogs. Sheep too.

If Oliver had decided to stay in Cambridge to research limbs in birds, it would have seemed much more interesting to John! He was really only joking when he laughed at Oliver's choice of research. He knew that all aspects of study are important.

Oliver completed the doctorate, but did not pursue a career in science. As we have seen, he instead joined the Inter-Varsity Fellowship, and spent his whole working life among students. For Oliver, as for John, students were a special group. They weren't more important than other people. God's love for poor people and for uneducated people is just as great as his love for students. So why did these two friends give so much energy all their lives to students?

Students will soon become schoolteachers, doctors, lawyers, lecturers, administrators, writers and journalists. Some will go on to serve in government. All these people influence the way others think. To change a nation, a good place to begin is the universities. This is the same all over the world.

When John spoke at university Christian Unions, he urged students to work hard, as he had in Cambridge. 'Your mind matters,' he would say. And he wrote a little booklet with that title.

Hundreds of students had come to hear John speak in Cambridge, soon after the holiday in Wales when he and John Collins discovered The Hookses. The CICCU arranged another mission four years later, and John returned there again. This time Billy Graham was leading the mission, with Uncle John as his chief assistant. John Stott and Billy Graham each had great respect for the other. One student said he saw them go round and round in the revolving door of the University Arms Hotel, where they were both staying. Each was deferring to the other, so neither wanted to get out first!

John Stott was soon travelling to many universities around the world to lead special mission weeks. 'We let him out on a long lead,' said one of his churchwardens.

Students from around the world

The British Empire steadily diminished in the 1960s as countries under British rule gained their independence. In each place the Union Jack was lowered in a special ceremony, and the country's new flag raised in its place. This was always captured on the television news. Several countries in Africa gained independence in the 1960s.

Uncle John was alert to these political changes. But what did political events in Africa have to do with a church in the West End of London? John Stott saw the link. It was students! Independent nations needed good leadership in every aspect of society, so would want their best students to have a Western education. (This was highly-regarded then, and still is now.) So John could see that as more countries gained independence, more students would come to study in the West. He was praying about this on his Quiet Days.

But how would this affect a *church*? It is hardly a university offering degrees! While a church doesn't give degrees, it *could* bring the students the Word of Life! Some countries sending students to the West largely followed Islam, or Hinduism, or Buddhism. All Souls could work to share the gospel of Christ with students from these nations while they studied here. It could also welcome the students who arrived as Christians already.

By the mid-1960s students from all over Africa, and many parts of Asia were streaming through the airports. London University was becoming very multi-cultural. And so was the Polytechnic of Central London (now part of Westminster University), just a hundred yards from All Souls. Students arrived in the country knowing no-one, and feeling very cold in Britain's October weather. John began the All Souls International Fellowship, offering Christian friendship. All Souls soon became known for its welcome.

John Stott did not ask the question 'What do we need?' He always asked 'What will be needed in five and in ten years' time?' and 'How can we start preparing for that now?' First, he began to look for an extra member for the staff team to lead the International work. From here the work grew and grew.

But while students kept coming Sunday by Sunday to All Souls, invitations also kept arriving for Uncle John to speak in universities around the world.

South Africa: aeroplane and atheists

Two of the best-known universities on the African continent are in South Africa. They are the University of Cape Town, and Witwatersrand [Wits] University in Johannesburg. In 1959 Uncle John led missions at both.

In Cape Town the students were very creative. One day they hired an aeroplane to swoop low across the campus, and drop leaflets about the mission! Everyone knew the mission was happening. Everyone was talking about it. Each evening, hundreds came to hear Uncle John speak.

A few days later John flew to Johannesburg. Here he was welcomed by Robin Wells, Chairman of the mission committee. John liked to live in the students' halls of residence during a mission, and was always grateful when one of the student leaders slept on someone else's floor for the week, to enable this. The Wits students knew this.

First Uncle John and Robin sat down over a cup of tea, before meeting with John Nowlan, the President of the Christian Union, and other student leaders. This was Uncle John's pattern wherever he led a university mission. He talked with the student leaders, and learned from them. They knew the university and had prayed for their fellow students; he was their servant for the week.

Robin John Nowlan has moved out of his room for you.

UJ That's kind of him. I know it's an upheaval, and I'm very grateful. I believe you're coming to London to study.

Robin Yes, that's right. My wife, Val, and I sail just a few days after the mission finishes. I have a place at Imperial College.

UJ I look forward to introducing you to my friend Oliver Barclay. He's on the staff of the Inter-Varsity Fellowship. Another scientist. You'll get on well.

John always enjoyed the chance to introduce his friends to others. Robin needed to brief John for the week ahead, but first he was keen to hear news of the Cape Town mission.

Robin How was your time in Cape Town? We were praying for the mission there.

It was good to hear a first-hand report from John's perspective, and to know so many students had come to meetings. Robin laughed when he heard about the aeroplane.

Robin Our Christian fellowship is smaller. Around half of Wits University is Jewish, and we have a strong Atheist Society. It can be quite aggressive.

UJ That's helpful to know. And you think the atheists could be active this week?

Robin It's likely. *[Then he added with a glint in his eye]* So everyone will know about the mission!

John laughed. It sounded as if God would use the atheists to bring glory to his Name.

UJ Now tell me how you want the meetings to end.

Robin We'd like to invite students who want to profess faith in Christ, or just want to find out more, to come to the front. We'll have older Christians there to talk with them. Local ministers and missionaries are coming to help.

John's mind often went back to the Sunday afternoon at Rugby when Bash urged that the boys *do* something with Christ.

UJ Good. I am glad you want to do that.

The atheists were indeed active. One day they handed out hundreds of leaflets, saying it was nonsense that Jesus was raised from the dead. The leaflets got everywhere – they were pushed under doors in the residences, laid out on tables in the refectory, and handed to students as they came out of lectures. God used the atheists to make sure everyone knew about the mission.

Uncle John spoke at lunchtime meetings, and each evening in the Great Hall, an impressive Greek-styled building with a grand flight of steps. He gave clear reasons for the Christian faith, drawing from the Old and New Testaments. Jews and atheists alike found a man who engaged with them and with their questions.

As often happens on university missions, numbers at the Wits meetings grew as the week progressed. By the middle of the week the atheists could contain themselves no longer. They arrived with banners that read, 'You lie!' and 'There is no God!' and 'God is Dead!'

Roy Comrie, a student at the time, tells what happened:

> First they marched quietly up and down the aisles, but we were all so captivated by what John Stott was saying that no-one noticed. So they began to shout.
>
> Uncle John stopped. Everyone wondered what would happen. Then after a pause, looking at the leader, John said 'Do come up to the platform,' and he invited him to the microphone!
>
> The atheist student was very bright, but totally disrespectful. He spoke to Uncle John as if he were an ignoramus.

Student *[aggressively]* I'll debate you on the existence of God.

UJ Very well. Let's do that. What about Saturday?

The debate was packed. The atheist proposer made 17 points. John Stott listened hard. Without taking any notes he stood up and dealt with all the points in order. He was gracious, patient and authoritative. Many lives were transformed that night. It was a great lesson for the Christian students to see what God can do.

The atheist leader did not become a Christian that week. Really thoughtful students often need more time to think carefully, and to count the cost of following Christ. 'Perhaps like Saul of Tarsus, he will one day preach the faith he's tried to destroy,' Uncle John reflected, as he wrote in his journal. Shortly afterwards he received news from the students that the Atheist Society had disbanded.

The Holy Spirit used John Stott to draw many to faith in missions like the ones in Cambridge, Cape Town and Wits. For Christian students, a mission like this strengthened their faith and helped them to be more courageous in speaking of it.

A few days after the Wits mission finished, Robin and Val began their journey to England. It had been a very busy time, with planning the mission, then packing, and saying goodbyes. Before they caught the boat, they first had a long train journey to Cape Town. John joined Robin's parents, Will and Lorna Wells, on the railway station platform to wave goodbye. He had enjoyed getting to know Robin and observing the way he led the student team. Uncle John sensed he would make a fine contribution to the Christian Union in London.

Soon the train drew in and Robin and his father heaved the suitcases into the carriage. After hugs goodbye, Robin and Val climbed on board, and the guard's whistle blew. Will, Lorna and John waved until the train turned a bend.

It was Uncle John's first time in Africa. Will and Lorna knew of his passion for birdwatching, and had made plans. 'You need to see our beautiful bird life,' said Will. 'We're taking you to Kruger National Park.' John was thrilled. Kruger is known across the world for Africa's 'big five' (lions, leopards, elephants, rhinos and buffalos), and for its stunning birds. With two weeks of university missions behind him, John was thankful for the chance to relax before flying home. That afternoon he cleaned the lenses of his binoculars and stuffed his washbag and a change of clothes into his rucksack. John Stott was off to Kruger, and he knew he would not be disappointed.

Three years later, in 1962, John was back in Africa for another speaking tour. It was as tightly-packed as ever. He started in Sierra Leone, then Ghana, Nigeria,

Kenya, Uganda and Zambia. With Frances's help, Uncle John had arranged many meetings, many conversations. Much travel had been put in place, by car, train and plane. It was in Kenya that he first met David Gitari, as a young student, several years before David stayed at the Wreckage.

    David Welcome to Kenya! We're delighted to have you here.

    UJ It's wonderful to meet you. I've been looking forward to it.

When Uncle John had had a chance to rest, they talked over a meal.

    David We have to tell you that things could get tough this week.

    UJ We never expect missions to be easy. But what's on your mind? Something in particular? [Uncle John could see the young student was troubled.] Is it Kenya's wait for independence? Will my Englishness count against me?

    David Yes. Partly your Englishness, and partly as you are a chaplain to the Queen. News has got out. It may not go down well here.

Not many students came to Christ that week. But the fruit of the mission could be seen a long time later. Years afterwards, David Gitari became Archbishop of Kenya, and could see the ripple effect of the mission across the church. But some time before that, over his breakfast with Uncle John in the Wreckage, he had some news to bring: 'Uncle John, he said, 'You exploded a myth in my university. You showed that Christianity is not cultural. So many Kenyan students think they are Christians just because they are not Muslims.'

Long trips away from home are demanding, especially when they cover several countries. The food is different from home, and the heat can be hard to cope with. But it was vital ministry, which God was blessing, and John Stott welcomed every opportunity he received. He had an unusual memory for names, and he needed it! He tried hard to remember everyone he talked with. 'I just love these Africans,' he wrote in his journal. 'They're so much more warm and open and sincere than Europeans.'

The following summer John was off on his 'long lead' from All Souls once again. This time he was flying to Asia. His mother wasn't well, but Joy managed to bring her to the airport to say goodbye.

John You've got my flight itinerary, Joy, haven't you?

Joy Yes. It looks exhausting. Eight countries!

Uncle John was to lead university missions in India, Malaysia, Singapore and the Philippines. Frances also lined up visits to All Souls missionaries and to church leaders in Iran, Sri Lanka, Hong Kong and Thailand.

John And you've got all the addresses where I'm staying?

John could not receive an email pushed through to his iphone, as would happen now. There was no email; there were no iphones. So he was always careful to give a street address where he knew it in advance, especially now his mother was more frail.

John I'll stay in touch as much as I can.

John kissed his sister and his mother goodbye, and picked up his briefcase, jammed with books and papers to read in-flight. It wasn't easy to leave family for these trips. He turned to wave goodbye again just before disappearing through the big doors marked 'DEPARTURES'. They waved back, and then made their way to the car park, glad to have seen him off.

Some weeks later Lily Stott suffered a stroke. Joy sent John a telegram straight away. But the telegram took six days to reach him, as he had left the address just before it was delivered, and he was now in Hong Kong. When the news caught up with him, John was shocked to receive it. Then further problems arose. He could neither send a telegram in reply, nor make a phone call. Because of severe storms, there was a breakdown of all telephone communication between Hong Kong and England. All he could do was to wait for more information.

John prayed much for his mother, and for Joy and Joanna, as he waited. Lily improved, though never fully recovered. Being away at times like this was a hidden cost of all the travelling. John was so grateful to Joy. She lovingly looked after both his parents as they got older.

Back home John Stott's links with the Christian Unions remained as strong as ever. Oliver Barclay took over the leadership of the Inter-Varsity Fellowship when DJ retired, and led the movement until 1980. Its publishing house, IVP, became the main publisher for John Stott's books. When Oliver retired, he was succeeded by Robin Wells. Robin had returned to South Africa after completing his doctorate at Imperial College and was by that stage a scientific advisor to the South African Government. But like John and Oliver, he remained deeply committed to students. So when the invitation arrived to succeed Oliver, he and Val decided that he should leave his role in Pretoria and bring their family over to the UK.

'Ah, Robin,' said John with evident approval when he heard news of the appointment. John had been struck by the clarity of Robin's thinking as a young man, and by the breadth of his theological reading. And as Uncle John spoke, something else was going through his mind. He had another new idea brewing, and from what he knew of Robin, he was sure Robin would want students involved in it. As soon as Robin settled into the role, John would talk with him about it.

Fascinating Fact 17

UNIVERSITY MISSIONS

Uncle John loved university missions, when the Christian gospel would become a talking point for students across the campus. He taught the Bible, night by night, often to large crowds, addressing questions like 'Who is Jesus?' and 'Why did he come to earth?' and 'What does he demand?'

He also answered questions the students raised. They wanted to know what Christianity had to do with science or philosophy or the environment. Uncle John listened carefully to each question. Then through gentle reasoning, he showed the students what the Bible said about these areas. A very similar pattern for university missions still exists now.

Always, always, *always* the cross of Christ was at the centre of his message. John Stott didn't just want students to know what the Bible taught on this area or that. He wanted students to come to Christ, truly sorry for their sin, and to find forgiveness, and a living faith, as he himself had at Rugby School.

Fascinating Fact 18

SHARP THINKERS

One of the many groups Uncle John started was called Christian Debate. This small group, all personally invited, met three times a year. Often they would read a book and discuss it. Christian Debate was made up of some of John Stott's sharpest friends. He had known most of them since they were students. The intellectual rigour of the discussions fed into John's own writing, and into the writing of the group members. Oliver Barclay and Robin Wells were both part of Christian Debate. It met in Uncle John's flat until he was almost eighty years old.

Fascinating Fact 19

SURPRISE IN SYDNEY

Leading a mission in Australia, at Sydney University, brought an unexpected outcome. John Stott was asked to explore the idea of becoming Archbishop of Sydney! The Australians sent telegrams to urge him to let his name go forward. He was very reluctant. His father had just died and he did not want to be so far from his elderly mother. The work at All Souls was proving very fruitful. In addition, the Australians had a very gifted candidate in Sir Marcus Loane. John felt Marcus Loane was their man. He wrote a careful letter then also sent a telegram, in as few words as possible:

WILLING NOMINATED BUT UNLIKELY ACCEPT IF ELECTED SUPPORT LOANE

Marcus Loane *was* elected, and John Stott became the more sure that he should not be in such a role.

Photo captions continued

19 On holiday with John Collins, 1952
20 With Billy Graham, Christmas 1956
21 Major-General Arnold Stott in Second World War
21 The young Rector, late 1940s
23 With Her Majesty the Queen Mother at All Souls, Christmas 1955
24 Talking with King Penguins, South Georgia Island, South Atlantic, 1991
25 Sir Arnold and Lady Stott, early 1950s
26 'Frances-the-omnicompetent' at her desk
27 With two former Study Assistants, Mark Labberton and Tom Cooper
28 With Nishi tribespeople at the Evangelical Fellowship of India conference, 1975
29 With Metropolitan Alexander Mar Thoma, Kerala, India, 1999
30 Laying concrete at The Hookses for the 'Frances Whitehead Walkway', 1992
31 Talking with a Royal Albatross chick, near Christchurch, New Zealand
32 John Stott at The Hookses, outside The Hermitage window
33 The Hookses, showing the bay. The Hermitage is bottom left
34 With Billy Graham before Billy's 406th crusade, in St Louis, 1999
35 With friends Saúl and Pilar Cruz, Mexico, 1999
36 Launching *The Cross of Christ* with IVP Publisher Frank Entwistle, 1986
37 Doctor of Divinity (DD) from London School of Theology, with Derek Tidball (Principal) and Frances Whitehead
38 John Stott with Corey Widmer (a Study Assistant) and Frances Whitehead
39 At home in London
40 With friend and biographer, Bishop Timothy Dudley-Smith
41 After receiving CBE at Buckingham Palace, with Frances Whitehead
42 At The Hookses with the grandchildren of friends, George and Maureen Swannell

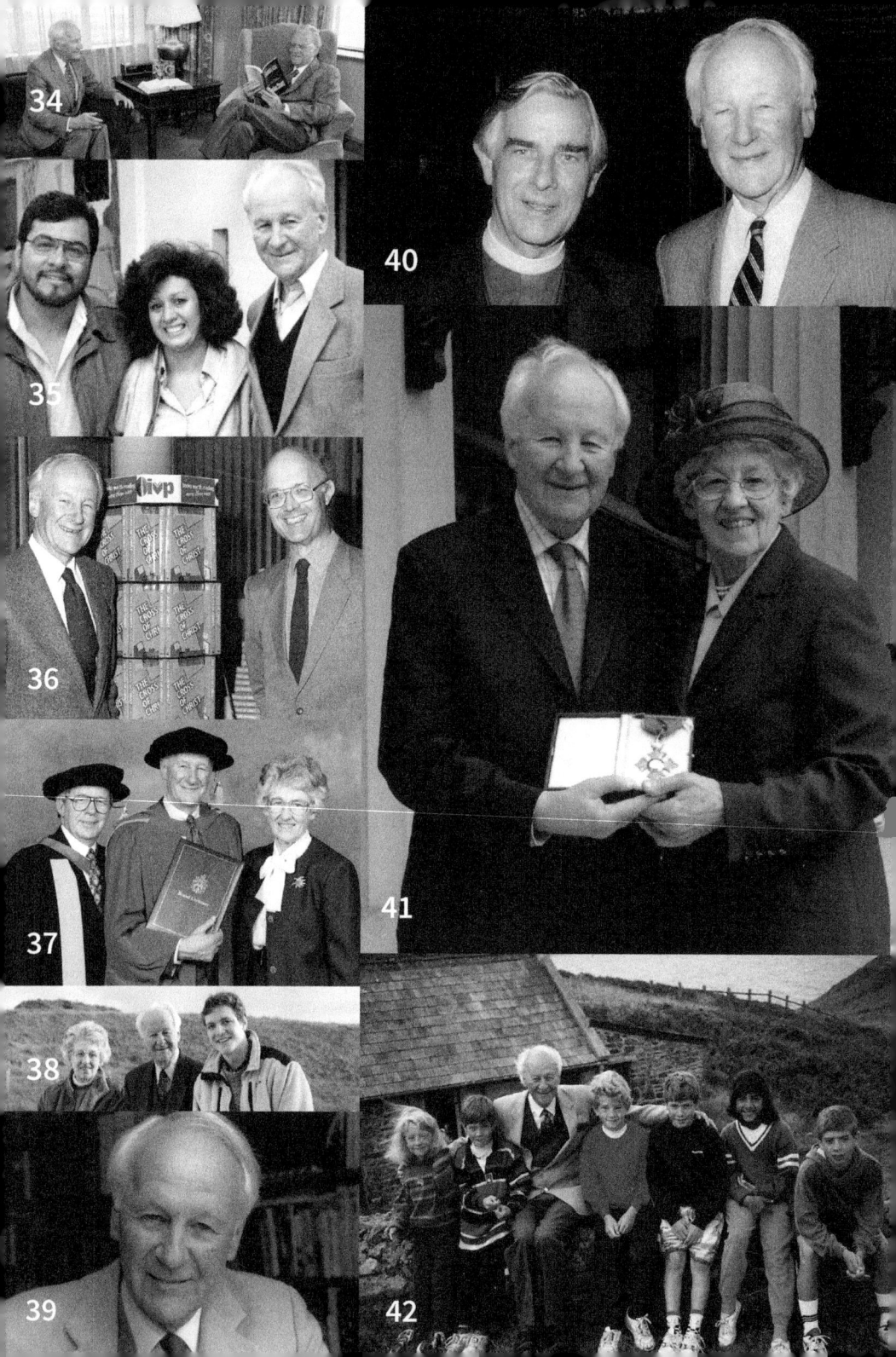

CHAPTER 10
THE WORLDWIDE CHURCH

We have heard how the Australians wanted Uncle John to be Archbishop of Sydney. The Aussies didn't give up, and they tried again in 1981. Uncle John talked with his small group of advisors. He met with the group regularly. 'Our Australian brethren have written again about my becoming a bishop,' he told them. 'Please let me know honestly what you think.'

Uncle John had already given the matter much prayer. He was deeply committed to the Anglican Church. If he accepted, he would become a member of the Lambeth Conference. This is a meeting of all Bishops and Archbishops from the whole Anglican church around the world. It is at Lambeth that direction is set and priorities decided. He would be able to speak into these discussions.

He was glad of the chance to discuss the matter with these old friends. They were advisors, but they were more. Uncle John called the meeting AGE. It stood for 'Accountability Group of Elders'. Uncle John placed himself under their leadership. He didn't want to be a free-floater who made his own decisions. That can lead to bad mistakes, where we think we have discerned God's will, but we haven't. 'There is wisdom in the counsel of many advisers,' (Proverbs 11:14) John often reminded himself. He would follow AGE's direction.

'John, you would be badly missed here if you went,' they said. 'And what about your new big idea?

John Stott's new idea was the London Institute for Contemporary Christianity. It would be based in St Peter's Church in Vere Street. His friends were right. It probably *did* need him in London to get it off the ground. So he wrote back to his good friends in Sydney, and he again graciously declined their invitation to become a bishop.

The London Institute was to open its doors the following year. John gave much time to explaining his dream for this when he travelled.

'I'm inviting some of the best young Christian leaders from around the world to come to London for ten weeks,' he began. 'We'll begin each day with Bible teaching. Then we will look at how to apply the Bible to some of the toughest questions in the world.'

The London Institute takes shape

John Stott had enjoyed conversations with students in Christian Unions on all six continents. He had sharpened their thinking, and they had expanded his. Soon these students would be graduates in the working world. In his mind's eye as he spoke, John could see their faces. He had got to know some of them quite well, but they did not know each other. In the London Institute they would meet each other. His young Latin American friends would meet his Asian friends; his European friends would meet his African friends. He was looking forward to it with a great sense of anticipation.

Uncle John always thought globally. 'Christ gave gifts to his church to share,' he would say. 'The church in each continent has been given different insights into scripture.' Through seminars, and discussion over meals, these insights would be shared.

'Could we arrange to meet?' John asked Robin Wells when he had settled into his new role. 'It would be good to see you again. And I have an idea I'd like to discuss with you.' They sat over a cup of tea in John's flat, as he outlined his hopes for the Institute. 'I very much want to see UK students and young graduates drawn in,' John said.

One of Robin's favourite phrases was 'iron sharpens iron' (Proverbs 27:17). He loved to help to sharpen students' thinking, so that they thought more clearly and more biblically. The Institute would do this in an international context. Robin warmed to John's idea, and took it to his staff and student leaders. Everyone was on board.

The London Institute for Contemporary Christianity opened in 1982. It is still to be found in the same building, with a bookshop open to the public, just a minute's walk from Bond Street tube station. It now offers courses online. The London Institute helps Christians to think biblically about their work, and about politics and about society. It stands as another part of Uncle John's legacy.

In 1985 Frances once again opened a letter with a crest on the envelope, this time from 10 Downing Street. The letter invited John Stott to become Bishop of Winchester. He was now 64 years old. Frances sensed she knew how he would respond.

The See of Winchester would also give Uncle John a seat in the House of Lords. Should he accept? Again he sought advice from friends. By now, he and his friends felt that his life was set in another direction. Once more he declined.

In one way it is surprising that it took so long for John Stott to be approached for a See (as a Bishop's area is called) in Britain. But in another way it is not surprising. Uncle John was a prominent evangelical leader. It could be uncomfortable to have him in discussions, as he would always want to be led by the Bible.

John Stott travelled around the world for over 50 years. That may sound very exciting. Indeed it *is* exciting, and a great privilege to see many countries. But it is also demanding. When you travel from East to West, you land in a country with your 'body clock' several hours out of sync. Jetlag can last three or four days at least. It's difficult to get to sleep, and then you wake up very early, while your body clock catches up with the actual time in the new country. Travelling from North to South (for example Europe to Africa) does not bring jetlag, but you still lose a night's sleep, unless you can sleep on a plane, which is not so easy in economy class. This is where Uncle John travelled, unless he got a free upgrade. Economy class saved a lot of money, and as others were covering travel costs, he did not want to burden them with extra expense.

When Uncle John was 84 years old, he received an invitation to visit China again. He raised the matter with his group of advisors. The church in China was growing very fast, as it still is now. It was clear he would love to go. 'Only if you have a medical doctor travelling with you,' said John Wyatt, his long-time friend and medical advisor. John thought and prayed about this. A few days later he surprised an old friend in Oxford with a call.

(Phone ringing)

Jonathan Hello, Jonathan West speaking.

> **UJ** Hello Jonathan. It's John Stott here.

Jonathan What a delight to hear you, John.

> **UJ** I'm phoning to ask a huge favour.

John had known Jonathan West since Jonathan was a schoolboy at camp, and he had preached at Jonathan's wedding to Virginia. The Wests were mission-minded Christians. Uncle John outlined the situation, and ventured to Jonathan the idea of the trip.

Jonathan I retired more than ten years ago. And I'm no expert in Asian fevers. But I'd love to help.

Uncle John was well-aware that Jonathan had retired years earlier, but he also knew his old friend would bring spiritual encouragement as well as good medical advice.

> **UJ** So you'll come! That's what I hoped you'd say! It's going to be a busy trip. I want to introduce Chris Wright to the Chinese. Chris is taking over from me as leader of Langham Partnership. [This was the name of John Stott's ministries.]

Uncle John went on to explain who else would be travelling with them.

> **UJ** We'll be five altogether. As well as Chris, we'll have Mark Hunt from America, and David Cansdale, George Cansdale's son. He is Chairman of Langham Partnership now. We fly first to Shanghai, then get the train to Nanjing. Then we'll come back to Shanghai and fly to Hong Kong, then home.

Uncle John was beginning to get frail, but he was like Caleb and wanted to serve and to minister for as long as the Lord gave him strength. With Jonathan West's agreement, John could now confirm the plans.

Map showing John Stott's final overseas trip in 2006

We know a lot about Uncle John's travels, as he wrote a diary. His visits were always tightly-packed. In the airport lounge, as he was about to fly to another country, or fly home, he took the chance to get out his pen and record events and impressions. He had done this for years. When John's parents were alive, he sent these notes to them, so they could catch up on what he had been doing. Then his parents would put them into a new envelope, and send them to Frances Whitehead. Frances read them, and passed on news to friends of how their prayers had been used. Then on Uncle John's return, the notes would be ready for their third use – a report for All Souls Church. These diaries stretched to 150-200 pages every year.

The diaries included descriptions of people John met, of any birdwatching he managed to squeeze in, and of food and culture, films and books. They show clearly his two major priorities: students and pastors. Uncle John knew he couldn't do everything. He had to make choices. Apart from writing and preaching, he chose to invest most of his time in students and in pastors, as they in turn would invest in many others.

Fascinating Fact 20

WORLDWIDE MOVEMENTS

The following worldwide movements held special significance for John Stott, to serve students, and to serve pastors.

IFES: Uncle John was a lifelong Ambassador-at-Large for the International Fellowship of Evangelical Students. (IFES). IFES links together all the Christian Unions in the world. Groups like the CICCU, which had helped John so much, are found in over 160 nations. John Stott knew many staff and student leaders in these groups by name, and loved to share fellowship with them. Douglas Johnson, Oliver's boss at the time, played a key role in founding IFES the year after John left Cambridge.

EFAC: Uncle John founded the Evangelical Fellowship in the Anglican Communion (EFAC) when he was 40 years old. It showed wonderful foresight and in a sense it was the forerunner of Langham Partnership. It continues to build national networks (like the Church of England Evangelical Council in England) and to provide fellowship for Anglican church leaders who love to teach the Bible. Liberal teaching in the church can leave evangelicals quite isolated in some areas.

Langham Partnership: John Stott was Founder and lifelong President of Langham Partnership International. Langham Partnership (i) provides books for pastors in the developing world, so they can study; and (ii) trains pastors in how to teach the Bible better, running 'Preaching Clubs' for them to help and encourage one another. In addition it (iii) raises funds to give scholarships to some of the best young Asian and African theologians, so they can pursue studies in the West. A few of them study at Tyndale House. John Stott invited Chris Wright to be its first International Ministries Director.

In addition came the Lausanne Movement. More about that in the next chapter.

Fascinating Fact 21

THE CHURCH IN CHINA

The church in China has grown massively. After the Communists came to power in 1949, all the missionaries had to leave. But this did not stop God's work in that mighty land. There have been periods of great persecution for the Chinese church, all faced with much courage. Christians in China now number around 100 million.

CHAPTER 11

FOCUS ON THE LAUSANNE MOVEMENT (EARLY 1970'S)

One afternoon, Uncle John received an unexpected call, which Frances was pleased to put through straight away. At the other end of the phone was a familiar American voice. It was John Stott's old friend, the evangelist Billy Graham. The conversation went something like this:

> **Billy Graham** John, I want to share an idea with you. What do you think of a plan to gather leaders from the whole evangelical church, for a Congress?'

Billy outlined his thinking. So much had changed in the world, and so quickly, since the Second World War. There was a lot for the church to talk about. Billy had called a meeting in Berlin in 1966 in which John Stott had played a major role. This was a kind of follow-up idea.

> **Billy Graham** The Congress will be held in 1974 and last for about ten days. We're thinking of holding it in Lausanne. It's a beautiful city on Lake Geneva. You probably know it.
>
> **UJ** Yes, I do know Lausanne. Tell me a bit more.
>
> **Billy Graham** It will focus on the church's main task, world evangelization. We need to keep the main thing the main thing. I think we could draw leaders from around 160 nations. I'm asking Jack Dain from Sydney to be Chairman.

John warmed to the idea of the event. He knew Bishop Jack Dain from his visits to Australia, and he sensed this could be important.

Billy Graham John, I've a question for you. I know it's a big ask.

UJ I'm listening. What's your big ask?

Billy Graham It's *listening*!

Billy Graham picked up on John's word, and laughed. Then he went on to explain:

> I want you to lead a small team to listen carefully to all the discussions. Then I'm thinking you would draw together a document to reflect all the voices you heard. That way it would be a document from the whole evangelical church.

John had theological weight and was a fine craftsman in the way he wrote. That was why Billy Graham's mind went straight to him for this major task. He would need to work with a core team, drawn from different countries. As he computed the task in his mind, Billy Graham anticipated his questions.

Billy Graham I'd love to see you work with Samuel Escobar from Peru, and Hudson Armerding.

John Stott knew these men well. The Latinos, and the Spanish-speaking world, would be particularly glad to have Samuel Escobar on the drafting committee. Sammy Escobar was deeply involved with student work. And Hudson Armerding, President of Wheaton College, near Chicago, also commanded great respect.

Two years later, on the last afternoon of the first Lausanne Congress on World Evangelization, John Stott presented the work of his 'listening' group. They had worked day and night, reading hundreds of notes sent to them by Congress participants.

The document was called *The Lausanne Covenant* - as it was a covenant with God, and a covenant with one another. This Covenant came to be regarded as one of the most significant documents in modern church history. From here a new movement was born. It took its name from the city where the first Congress took place, and is still known as the Lausanne Movement.

A second Lausanne Congress was held in Manila, Philippines, in 1989. John Stott was there, and he shaped *The Manila Manifesto* which came out of it. This built on *The Lausanne Covenant*.

Now let's fast forward to The Third Lausanne Congress on World Evangelization. In 2006, before the planning for this Congress began, Doug Birdsall, Chairman of the Lausanne Movement, called John Stott. They arranged to meet for dinner in a small Greek restaurant near Uncle John's flat. Doug wanted advice. He sensed it was time to bring the Church together again, as so much had changed since the last Congress: Communism had all but collapsed; everyone now used computers and mobile phones; 9/11 had opened a new age of religious terrorism. Life was completely different, and the church faced new pressures.

The church had grown wonderfully in the previous two decades. The Lausanne Movement would now have to span 200 nations. 'It will be a huge task,' said John. 'Yet I believe we must do it.'

After dinner, they made their way back to Uncle John's flat. He was now 85 years old, walking slowly, holding onto Doug's arm with one hand, and holding his cane with the other. 'I just hope I live long enough to see all this come to pass,' he said as they parted.

The following year Uncle John moved into a home for retired clergy just outside London. He was frail, but his passion did not diminish. John Stott was delighted when he heard the news that Lindsay Brown would serve as International Director of the Lausanne Movement. John had first met Lindsay when Lindsay was studying history at Oxford, and was president of the university Christian Union. Lindsay, just like Oliver, gave his life to working with students. John knew Lindsay and Doug would make a strong team, and he prayed for them.

Lindsay Brown invited a group of theologians from around the world to lay plans for the statement which would come out of the third Congress.

> **Lindsay Brown** This statement will stand in the historic line of *The Lausanne Covenant*. The first half will set out our evangelical convictions, as all we do comes from what we believe. The second part will be a call to action for the whole evangelical church.

The group Lindsay brought together included Chris Wright, John Piper, Sinclair Ferguson, Peter Jensen, Rose Dowsett, Ajith Fernando, and several of John's other friends. 'We've had a *Covenant* and a *Manifesto*. What shall we call the statement this time?' someone asked.

Chris Wright What about *The Cape Town Commitment*? It has good alliteration, and it says exactly what it is.

There were nods of approval all around the room and the name was agreed.

The first meeting of these theologians was held in Minneapolis. Chris took careful notes on his laptop, listening intently to everyone in the room. As he flew back to London, he screened down the notes. He had been asked to craft the statement, and he would need the Lord's special help to fashion the outline. It was a huge responsibility.

A month later, Chris drove to The Hookses. He often went there to write, sitting at John's desk overlooking the bay. As Chris was driving down the motorway, he was thinking and praying about how the *Commitment* should be shaped. Chris knew how much John Stott cared about the Lausanne Movement, and he called him when he reached The Hookses.

Chris Wright As I've been praying, driving down here, I've been thinking about God's covenant love for us, and our love for God. This could form the backbone of *The Cape Town Commitment*. What do you think?

UJ Then would there be a call to action coming out of this? Have I remembered rightly?

Chris Wright Yes, that's right. A Confession of Faith followed by a Call to Action.

UJ I like your plan. It has a freshness about it. And there is no better basis for action than God's love.

John had preached until he could preach no longer. In his final public address, at the age of 86, he had urged Christians to be more like Christ, who embodied truth and love. *The Cape Town Commitment* would continue to urge Christians to a life of love.

In February 2011, four months after the Congress, the phone rang in Uncle John's room in the middle of the afternoon. It was Doug Birdsall, calling from Boston. By this stage John had become very frail, but his mind was still keen. Phillip Herbert, an old friend, was with him.

Phillip Hello. John Stott's room.

Doug It's Doug Birdsall here.

Phillip What a coincidence! We're just reading *The Cape Town Commitment*. Let me pass over the phone.

Frances Whitehead had brought Uncle John a copy of the newly-published *Commitment* a few days earlier. Phillip was reading it slowly and carefully, so Uncle John could take in every phrase. He spoke into the phone in a weak and halting way:

UJ I'm pleased to hear your voice, Doug. It's a beautiful and profound document. With it, you seem to have achieved an astonishing degree of unity.

This unity was what John Stott had been praying for. He knew that thousands of ministries and churches would adopt the *Commitment*, and he saw the vital importance of getting it right.

Fascinating Fact 22

CARING FOR POOR PEOPLE

John Stott saw from scripture that God's people everywhere should care for the last, the least and the lost. From 1983-1997 he served as President of Tearfund, the evangelical relief and development agency.

In 1992 Uncle John visited the work of four former students of the London Institute in Mexico. Sergio and Hortensia Sánchez had set up a ministry among eighty Indian communities, responding to deep social needs in the name of Jesus Christ. Saúl and Pilar Cruz served in Jalalpa, a gigantic slum in Mexico City where three million people lived in shacks made out of cardboard and milk cartons. They set up self-help programmes to enable people to build better houses, and formed children's clubs. They named their organization ARMONIA, meaning harmony. By expressing Christ's love in these ways, all four were also able to teach about his salvation. Uncle John was thrilled to see what they were doing.

Two years later, in South India, John met Mercy Abraham, a young Christian woman with a passion to help abused and abandoned women. Moved by the stories she shared, he invited her to London. As she spoke at All Souls, everyone listened intently. With gifts from John Stott and London friends, she purchased land in Dharmapuri for what is now the Mahalir Aran Trust (which means 'a fortress for women'). It has since built its own chapel, it farms its own land, and it has founded a clinic to serve 400 poor families in surrounding villages. It also supports local pastors and their families to serve these villages. Mercy has built a small tradecraft factory to provide employment for the women, teaching them skills to make fabric and jewellery products for sale in the West. The Mahalir Aran Trust has helped hundreds of women, and saved baby girls from being killed. John Stott was 73 years old when he first met Mercy. He never stopped encouraging Christians to demonstrate their faith in practical ways.

Fascinating Fact 23

ON A LIGHTER NOTE

It's not always easy to remember who did what. Here's an easy way to remember the names of those who worked with John Stott on the 1974 drafting committee for the Lausanne Covenant. Samuel Escobar comes from Peru, and that's also where Paddington Bear came from. Hudson Taylor Armerding, named after Hudson Taylor, the famous missionary to China, was President of Wheaton College. The original wardrobe from *The Lion, the Witch and the Wardrobe* is at Wheaton College. There is a notice on it to say that no responsibility will be taken for anyone who climbs through it.

Chapter 12

John Stott: The Man Himself

'I can hear the chains clanking from here,' Joy used to tease her brother. 'Johnnie, you're a slave-driver!'

John Stott worked very hard. Those on his team had to work hard too, to keep up. Was he a slave driver? Not really!

In this final chapter we get a few more glimpses behind the scenes. They come from friends who worked with him at different points in his life. But first, here is the story of how Uncle John's life came to be captured in print.

Richard Bewes, then Rector of All Souls Church, was talking with John Stott and his Advisory Group of Elders. The conversation went something like this.

Richard I'd like to make a suggestion. I've already talked with John about it, as I didn't want to take him by surprise in the meeting.

It's always good to prepare for a meeting in this way, to save surprises. From the way Richard was speaking, he clearly had an important matter on his mind. Everyone was listening hard. What would his suggestion be?

Richard I think we should ask someone write a biography of John.

Others That sounds an interesting idea.

I think it's a good idea, while people's memories are fresh.

And it'll mean we have a true account from which others can draw if they are writing about you, John.

Richard Yes, that's *exactly* what lies behind my thinking. There will be several books about John in the future, perhaps many. We need to capture your life, John, while you yourself can remember things, and by talking with people who know you.

UJ I hope it can wait to be published until I'm in heaven.

Richard That's in the Lord's hands, John. But we should start work soon, as it will take a long time to write.

Others Do you have a writer in mind?

He would need to have a good sense of history, and know John personally.

And he'd need to have time. And to write well.

Richard You're right. He would need all these things. I wonder about Bishop Timothy Dudley-Smith. He is due to retire next year. He fits all the categories, and people know his name through the hymns he's written. Should I sound him out? What are your thoughts?

And so it was that Richard Bewes wrote to Bishop Timothy on behalf of AGE. It would be a huge undertaking. Bishop Timothy and his wife, Arlette, thought and prayed about it. Ten years or so later, after much work and many interviews with people who knew Uncle John, two massive volumes were published, beautifully written, a total of 1,000 pages, with 450,000 words. Future historians will always have a debt of gratitude to Bishop Timothy Dudley-Smith for his diligent work.

Let's turn now to eleven stories about John Stott, the man himself.

1   He cared about international students

When Uncle John waved Robin and Val Wells off on their boat train to Cape Town, he made a mental note of when they would dock in Southampton. 'I'll surprise them,' he thought to himself. John flew back to London shortly after his trip to Kruger National Park. This meant he arrived home several days before they docked.
On a dull and cloudy morning, Robin and Val lugged their cases off *SS The Pretoria Castle*, and onto the train bound for London. The cases were heavy, with a lot of books. (In those days suitcases had no wheels.) It was the Wellses' first time in the UK. Everything is new to international students. The houses, the climate, the food, the money… An hour later, the train pulled into Waterloo. Now, with their heavy luggage, they would have to find their way to their flat. Or so they thought.

Stepping down onto the platform, they were amazed to hear a familiar voice. 'Robin! Val!'

There was Uncle John, walking towards them. 'Welcome to England!' he said with a warm handshake. 'I hope you've had a good voyage.' They were very touched that he should meet them. 'My jalopy's just outside', he added. John picked up one of the heavier cases, and they made their way to his van.

London can be an unwelcoming place on a dreary morning. But a welcoming smile soon changes that. John's little blue Austin was jammed to its limits. With one final heave, the back door clicked shut. John drove the Wellses to their flat.

John Stott often invited international students to the 'Wreckage'. He loved it when they got in touch. Some, like David Gitari, stayed for a time if there was room. Others just called in. 'Come and have an English cup of tea,' he would say to his friends as he travelled.

2   He liked to be punctual,
so as not to waste other people's time

When Uncle John was in America in 1964 to speak to students, his guide and companion for the trip, which included many meetings in universities, was

Keith Hunt (Mark Hunt's father). While based for a few days at Cedar Campus in the state of Wisconsin, Keith and Mark took John on an early-morning birding expedition. Uncle John had a meeting at 11am to discuss a new venture; so he needed to be back in good time to get washed and changed.

They set out early, with a canoe loaded onto the roof rack of Mark's Volkswagen Beetle, to hunt for the nesting site of the Common Loon (known in the UK as the Great Northern Diver). They had already tried a few days before, tramping through a swamp and swatting mosquitoes, but with no success.

First they visited the nearby lakes, but no loon was to be found.

'There's another lake up in that direction,' said Mark, pointing with a nod of his chin into the mid-distance. John looked at his watch. 'I daren't risk being late,' he said.

'We'll be fine,' the Hunts assured him. 'It isn't far.' Uncle John wasn't keen, but he had been overruled. They set off again, up a track, Mark's father in the passenger seat and John in the back. The track surface was poor, and filled with holes and rocks. Mark drove as carefully as he could but suddenly one of the tyres slipped off a large rock and there was a loud crunching sound. This was very bad news.

Mark scrambled under the car to find an engine mount had snapped, but the tyre was still intact. Could the car still be driven? The engine was continuing to run, so he got back in and pressed the clutch pedal. Now the engine raced. They decided to attempt their journey back to base. Somehow they managed to turn the car around. Each time Mark released the pedal, the engine slowed, but it was still going too fast for the kind of road they were on. As soon as they reached a better road, desperate to make up time, Mark pressed the clutch down again. Bouncing over holes, skidding around bends, and racing at terrible speeds on the better stretches, John was finally delivered back to Cedar Campus. It must have been terrifying!

'We're two minutes early, Uncle John!' said Mark, thankful for their safety and hugely relieved at the time they had made up. Uncle John piled out of the car to wash and change as quickly as he could. Mark knew he should not have insisted on the last lake when time was short. Anyone else might have shown impatience and even bad temper, but John Stott kept quiet, and he never referred to the incident again.

3   He liked accuracy

Before Windows-based software, people used typewriters which had no memory. So if a change was needed, a whole page had to be re-typed. If Frances spotted an error in something, she would often re-type a page. Then in the 1980s a massive change came about. The word processor took the place of the typewriter. Lord Sugar's new Amstrads appeared on office desks. No longer would a whole page ever need to be retyped again!

When John Stott was 85 years old, he dictated a letter to another elderly pastor, for Frances to type. Frances was typing fast, and her fingers slipped, so she inadvertently added an extra character. As Uncle John was reading through the letter before signing it, she heard very loud laughter. This is what John read:

'I too am still preaching, although I am now 875 years old.'

4   He urged Christians to live simply

He lived simply, as we have seen. If he had clothes he didn't wear, he gave them away. He kept his wardrobe to a minimum. He would be smartly dressed for meetings, and put on old clothes at The Hookses, apart from on Sundays for church. There was a time when he had only one pair of respectable shoes; if they needed to be repaired, they were repaired on a Saturday. He never, ever, accepted a second helping of food if he was out for a meal, and he had a second slice of toast and marmalade at breakfast only on Sundays – he was always determined to control his appetite.

5   He wanted his Study Assistants to grow spiritually

Bishop Toby Howarth was Study Assistant when Uncle John was in his mid-sixties. The Study Assistants helped with research, but in addition they did many practical things for John, and would also travel with him. John had invited some people from All Souls around for a meal, and the menu was to be kebabs, purchased from around the corner, followed by ice-cream and chocolate sauce.

'Have you remembered to buy the ice cream? Uncle John asked Toby that afternoon.

'Yes' said Toby, with his mind on something else. In fact he had *not* bought it, but he had made a mental note to do so. However Toby forgot to buy it, and when people finished their kebabs he suddenly remembered. It was too late… All the shops nearby were closed. So there was chocolate sauce, but no ice cream for it to go over. This was very embarrassing for Toby, and it was embarrassing for Uncle John as host.

The next morning Toby walked slowly up the stairs to Uncle John's sitting room to apologize. They talked through what happened, and how our behaviour as Christians relates to the character of God. Then they knelt on the floor and prayed together. Uncle John never mentioned the incident again.

6   He was a lifelong birdwatcher

We've heard about his search for the Common Loon. Uncle John saw 2,500 of the world's 9,000 bird species, and was expert in photographing them. Ornithology is the study of birds, but John's was the study of birds as part of God's majestic creation. It was, he joked, 'orni-theology'. He loved to teach theology from his birdwatching, and wrote *The Birds our Teachers* to do this.

7   He loved The Hookses

The Hookses remained a very special place to John Stott. He made his final trip there, aged 87. It held so many memories for him: writing books, laughing with friends, hard physical work, enjoying the stunning birdlife and seascapes. Jonathan West had accompanied him on his final overseas trip, to China, in 2006. Now, in the late summer of 2008, Jonathan and Virginia were with him on his final trip to The Hookses. Frances was there too, and a handful of other friends. John spent much time in The Hermitage, enjoying memories of the way the Lord had helped him write as he sat overlooking the bay. In the evenings Jonathan wheeled Uncle John's chair up the slope to the main house for supper together.

8   He kept the main thing the main thing

At the age of 81, John Stott was in India to help pastors in their preaching. His American Study Assistant Corey Widmer was travelling with him. While in Madras (also known as Chennai), the capital city of Tamil Nadu state, they had the chance to go birding on an afternoon off. That afternoon Uncle John tripped and fell, and cut his leg. Soon the wound became painful and swollen, and it had to be treated at a hospital. Corey was concerned, as it got worse rather than better. He eventually managed to talk on the phone with Uncle John's heart specialist in London. Advice was clear: unless it improved straight away, they should fly home.

Corey relayed the message to Uncle John, and both of them realized the seriousness of the matter. Their conversation did not get morbid. Far from it! John talked in his usual light-hearted manner, despite his pain; he was light-hearted but serious. He knew Corey wanted to become a pastor, and he wanted to impart some advice from his own experience.

'Above all, Corey,' Uncle John said, 'cling to the cross.' John Stott would talk of the Apostle Paul being 'obsessed' with the cross, and he adopted Galatians 6:14 as one of his 'life verses'. It was a verse to live by; a verse which should affect every aspect of his life. It reads:

> May I never boast except in the cross of our Lord Jesus Christ, through which the world has been crucified to me, and I to the world.

As we know, Uncle John did recover, and he had more years ahead of him in which to preach and teach and write. His advice that afternoon to Corey, which, as far as they knew then, could be one of their last times together, made a deep impression.

9   He wanted to show the fruit of the Holy Spirit in his life

> The fruit of the Spirit is love, joy, peace, patience, kindness, goodness, faithfulness, gentleness, self-control
> GALATIANS 5:21, 22

He knew that this could come only from the life of God in him. We have seen how he read the whole Bible each year. Before his Bible reading in the morning, he would greet the day by greeting the Lord. He would say, 'Good morning Heavenly Father, good morning Lord Jesus, good morning Holy Spirit'. It wasn't a matey 'hey there', but it showed how close he felt God to be. He went on to say to each Person in the Trinity that he worshipped them.

10   He prepared sermons with great care

John Stott was highly-experienced as a public speaker. Could he have entered the pulpit without much preparation? Yes and No. Yes, he could have spoken, and spoken well, without much thought. Like every schoolteacher, the more you teach, the less you have to prepare. But preaching is different. Uncle John sensed the weight of his responsibility to teach the word of God. As a rough guide, he reckoned on an hour's preparation for each minute of preaching. That may seem a long time. He wanted his hearers to get the most out of the Bible passage, and there were no shortcuts to that, so he studied hard, read widely, and prayed, to give them the best.

11   He was a radical

Uncle John's ministry was one of service, not of lording it over others. He became a friend to thousands around the world, enjoying fellowship when they met, and following as much news of them as he could. He prayed regularly for many people.

In some cultures John would have a garland hung around his neck, to express honour. He often addressed large crowds of people, and received applause. But he always remained a modest man, living simply, and owning very little.

We have seen some of the difficulties he had to face. He struggled with sin like we all do. But he didn't give up.

Radical means working from the roots. Uncle John was truly radical. He worked from the roots, and he himself was firmly rooted. His days were rooted in Christ from the moment he got out of bed, and said 'Good morning' to the Holy Trinity. This was the secret of his effectiveness.

Fascinating Fact 24

COMMANDER OF THE ORDER OF THE BRITISH EMPIRE (CBE)

In November 2005, John Stott was informed that his name would appear in the Queen's 2006 New Year's Honours List, as a Commander of the Order of the British Empire (CBE). Uncle John felt deeply honoured to receive this. An award always has what is called a 'citation' explaining what it is for. The citation read: *For services to Christian Scholarship and the Christian World.*

He wondered how friends around the world may react to an honour which speaks of the 'British Empire', as many of his friends were from countries which had gained independence from Britain forty or more years earlier.

John, Frances and Tyler Wigg-Stevenson, John's then Study Assistant, met together, as this trio often did. (John referred to them as 'the happy triumvirate'.) Between them they composed a message which would be emailed to all John's friends as soon as the announcement was made public. First it explained the British honours system and how it worked. Then John wrote: 'While I am grateful for the citation, I am somewhat embarrassed by reference to the British Empire which long ago ceased to exist!' There was no British superiority in John Stott's thinking.

Fascinating Fact 25

LOVE OF CREATION

John Stott did not accept honorary office of a movement unless he could participate in its life to some extent, or at least pray for it. We have seen his love of the natural world. In the early 1980s his friends Peter and Miranda Harris founded A Rocha, in Portugal, which grew from a Christian conservation centre into an international movement. He became thoroughly involved in it, accepting honorary office from its early days, visiting whenever he was able, and helping to fashion the direction it took. **arocha.org**

And Finally

John Stott died on the 27 July, 2011, with close family and friends at his bedside. As they sat with him, Handel's *Messiah* played quietly in the background. Uncle John loved the *Messiah*, and was often at the Albert Hall in London to hear it on Good Friday. 'I know that my Redeemer liveth' was as much his certainty, as it was the prophet Isaiah's certainty. One of the group read him verses from Paul's second letter to Timothy. He went to be with Christ in the middle of the afternoon. Within hours, this news spread across the world through social media.

BBC News 24 carried an announcement that evening, the *New York Times* published a tribute the following morning, and *The Times*, *The Independent*, *The Telegraph* and *The Guardian* all carried long obituaries on 29 July. A memorial website collected stories and tributes by their hundreds, and Thanksgiving services were planned across the world.

Hugh Palmer led Uncle John's funeral service in All Souls on 8 August that year. John Stott's niece, Caroline Bowerman, told movingly of how 'Uncle Johnnie' always had time for his family, even when other pressures were great. Toby Howarth related how, on a trip to India, Uncle John had found he was to preach in more churches than planned. They had to hop on a rickshaw straight after one service to get to another, to start again. It was tiring, especially in the heat. 'Remember we're here as servants,' John had said to Toby.

His Honour Judge David Turner, a member of AGE, reflected on John Stott as a friend, and long-time mentor. David had come to All Souls first in 1972 as a student. 'This is an "au revoir" occasion,' and you do not need firsts in French and theology from Cambridge to know what that means,' he said.

As an eighteen-year-old student, David Turner had been drawn to All Souls week by week to hear Uncle John's compelling preaching. It made a profound impact on him, he recalled, to see John kneel down to pray, and ask God's help, before he preached.

In a more light-hearted vein, he went on, 'I remember one day arriving at All Souls from court, for a meeting. I had been literally dive-bombed by a seagull as I walked up from Oxford Circus. I was dabbing at my suit and came in muttering 'wretched seagull'. John was unsympathetic!
   "A herring gull, a black-headed gull it may have been; a mere 'seagull'
   it was not! Dear brother, you have been judged for your ignorance!"
You did not mess with John when it came to birds!'

David Turner concluded: 'John was a man, and a minister, of sparkling intellect, rare graciousness and deep kindness; of disarming humility and disconcerting effectiveness. A ten-talent man. John joked about his "daily dogged discipline", but it made him who he was, under God.

'He had an uncanny gift for friendship, for deep encouragement, and for remembering names. Our debt to this great and good man is incalculable. It will reverberate in eternity. We will not forget him.'

At the London Memorial service the following January in St Paul's Cathedral, the Archbishops of Canterbury and York, and the Bishop of London were all present. At Uncle John's request, Bishop Timothy Dudley-Smith was the preacher. Strikingly, they did not wear their mitres or their ecclesiastical robes, out of honour for a man who carried no high office in the church.

> **Those who are wise will shine like the brightness of the heavens, and those who lead many to righteousness, like the stars for ever and ever.**
> **DANIEL 12:3**

What will John Stott's legacy be to the church? We will know better in forty or fifty years' time, and we will know perfectly in heaven.

Appendices

Questions for Book Clubs

Some readers have read this story in a book club, with friends. If you do that, the following questions may be useful to ponder.

1 Do you agree with Uncle John about the need to teach children spiritual truth? What lessons did you learn when you were younger, which lend strength to his argument? Uncle John felt it important for Christian children and teenagers to understand what they believe, so they can explain it. Do you understand what you believe well enough to 'make a case' for it?

2 John Stott thought no Christian should ever go to war. He did not realize this is an issue on which Christians may disagree. What other issues can you think of where the Bible gives liberty for different views?

3 Uncle John did not become a member of the CICCU, out of honour for his father, who asked him not to. And when Mr Earnshaw-Smith invited John to be a curate at All Souls, Langham Place, he asked for time to consult his father, even though his father wasn't a Christian. What can we learn from Uncle John about respect for parents?

4 John Stott showed unusual self-discipline from his days at school onwards. Are there areas of life where you could be more disciplined? Identify some goals with one or two friends - and then encourage each other to reach them and maintain them.

5 'If you don't use something for more than a year, it means you don't need it.' This was John Stott's very practical way of making decisions about what he should keep. What do you think of this way of making such decisions?

6 A pattern of investing in future leaders began to form in Uncle John's life. This is seen in where he gave his best energies: speaking at university missions, working with others to shape the Lausanne Movement; founding and leading the London Institute and Langham Partnership International – and writing books. Are we too impatient in wanting to see results from what we do?

7 John Stott led the way in caring for poor people while he was at Rugby School through the ABC club, and then in the All Souls parish. Years later, he was thrilled to see the initiatives taken by Sergio and Hortensia Sánchez and Saúl and Pilar Cruz in Mexico, and Mercy Abraham in India. Are there projects you could do locally to care for poor people?

8 When Mercy Abraham wrote to Uncle John, she always included the words 'A soldier of Jesus Christ' beside her signature. What can we learn from Ephesians 6:10-20 and 2 Timothy 2:3-4 about being a good soldier of Jesus Christ?

Three Ideas of Things To Do

If you have enjoyed this story, here are three ideas of things to do.

1. Listen to Uncle John preach. Go to **allsouls.org** and search for 'John Stott', then register (free) to download or listen on line to his sermons.

2. Start your own **Nature Notebook** and build a list of what you see. You may enjoy Uncle John's *The Birds our Teachers,* for which he took all the photographs himself. It took Uncle John 25 years to capture the prized Snowy Owl (photo 5). You will find the story in his book.

3. Consider reading the Bible through in one or two years, using the McCheyne reading plan which Uncle John used for 50 years. You will find it as a free download. Or it is published in *Authority and Joy: The Bible in your life* by John Stott and Sinclair Ferguson (Dictum, 2021), with a brief introductory note from Uncle John. It is the best-known reading plan in the world.

We opened this book with a group of friends crowding around a copy of *TIME* magazine in April 2005, and swapping their stories. You now know more than any of them did. They were surprised to see Uncle John's name in the list of top 100 influential people in the world. Would you have been surprised?

Who We Are

Dictum was founded in 2018, and is based in Oxford. It publishes books for the West and the Global South which are biblical, pastoral and incisive. Dictum's lists (opposite) include classic reprints. Churches or agencies ordering in bulk, perhaps for a special event or anniversary, are invited to add their logo and a description of their ministry at the front of titles purchased. Review copies are available at no charge. For more, visit *dictumpress.com*

The Evangelical Fellowship in the Anglican Communion (EFAC) was founded with prescience in 1961 by John Stott. EFAC works to enable Anglican leaders around the world to stand firm, to engage thoughtfully with secular trends, and to articulate a persuasive biblical response to them. Its Theology Resource Network (TRN) draws senior theologians from all continents. The Church of England Evangelical Council (CEEC) is its affiliated group in England. To learn more, and view their publications, visit *efacglobal.com* and *ceec.info*

Clarity and brevity are two great gifts to the world.

Dictum's books do not waste words, or waste the reader's time. They bring biblical thinking which is refreshing, clear and well-applied.

Dictum has four lists:

Dictum Essentials: Core books for wide use in churches and mission agencies, with questions for personal reflection or group discussion.

Oxbridge: Church history from the ancient university towns of Oxford and Cambridge. Including a Reformation Walking Tour; and a humorous feline view of Oxford.

Unique angles on John Stott's ministry, including the remarkable story of Frances Whitehead, his secretary for 55 years, a story which needs to be preserved; and a fun authorized children's biography.

List Four: A growing and diverse wider list of pithy books, longer and shorter.

dictumpress.com

books worth reading more than once

RELATED TITLES

Further titles written or edited by Julia Cameron
which bring insight on John Stott's ministry

John Stott's Right Hand
The untold story of Frances Whitehead
Dictum/EPAC, expanded and updated 2020

'It is widely agreed that John Stott would not have achieved half of what he did without Frances. Theirs was one of the greatest partnerships in Christian history.' (Chris Wright)

John Stott: Pastor, Leader and Friend
Dictum/EPAC, expanded and updated 2020

Foreword by Bishop Michael Nazir-Ali. Contributors include Chris Wright, Lindsay Brown, Bishop Henry Scriven, Bishop Timothy Dudley-Smith, Samuel Escobar for Latin America; Femi Adeleye and Daniel Bourdanné for Africa.

Charles Simeon on 'The Excellent Minister' as Mentor and Model
Dictum/EPAC, expanded and updated 2021

With Michael Rees and John Benton. This traces Simeon's influence through the present day. John Stott regarded Simeon as his mentor. A fine engraving of the famous 'Simeon silhouette' is also available. Uncle John and Frances Whitehead each had Simeon silhouettes hanging in their homes.